W9-BUR-398

3 0000 006 999 423
LIBRARY OF MICHIGAN

Lessons in Leadership from the Ground Up

TURNING
DREAMS
INTO
SUCCESS

Lessons in Leadership from the Ground Up

TURNING
DREAMS
INTO
SUCCESS

Bunny and Larry Holman

LESSONS IN LEADERSHIP FROM THE GROUND UP:
Turning Dreams into Success
First Edition. Copyright © 1999 by Bunny and
Larry Holman. Printed in the United States.

All rights reserved.

Holman, Bunny and Larry.
        Lessons in leadership from the
ground up: turning dreams into success /
by Bunny and Larry Holman — 1st ed.
            "A Lesson in Leadership Book."
            ISBN: 0-9648829-9-X
1. Leadership.   2. Success.
3. Dreams.

10 9 8 7 6 5 4 3 2 1

HF
5386
.A65
1999

ACKNOWLEDGMENTS

T his book represents a dream as well—one shared by many dedicated people who offered up their own insights, enthusiasm, and talent to help make it a reality.

We'd like to thank the writing team of Adam Bruns (who focused on chapters featuring Jack Canfield, Joanne Everett, David Lyman, Tori Murden and Pat and Jean Smith); Vickie Mitchell (Steve Lambert, Joanna McGoldrick, Bob Voss); and Tom Wallace (Juliet Mee, Tom Roberts). We would especially like to thank WYNCOM's John McGill (Willie King, Harold Koning, Bill Phifer), who conceived the book's theme and served as editor and lead writer, guiding the project to completion with his considerable organizational skills, as well as his outstanding writing abilities.

In particular, we are grateful to our college and university partners who put us in contact with many of the people you see profiled in these pages; and many others who are not featured here simply for lack of space. In no particular order, we would like to thank:

Chris Balling of the University of Utah

Camille Hassenplug of Columbus State University

Irene Hurst of the University of South Florida

Nancy Kinsey of the University of Texas at Arlington

Betty H. Anderson of McNeese University

Lisa Mitchell of Old Dominion University

Brad Heegel of Augustana College

Ann Tate of the University of Nevada-Las Vegas

Virginia Mee of Southwest Missouri State University

Paul Newlin of Penn State Erie

Ron Avillion of Penn State University

Sharon Scott of Virginia Tech

Connie Blakemore of the University of Kentucky

Stephanie Elders of Riverside Community College

Damaris Schlong of Amarillo College

Leigh Z. Rorschach of the University of Tulsa

Mildred B. Kelley of Jackson State University

Lee Nelson of the University of Texas at El Paso

Lori Holden Dowd of Colorado State University

Brenda McCoy of Franklin University

Dr. Sylvia Caceres of the University of Central Florida

Linda Godfrey of the University of Maine

Skye Myrick of Asheville-Buncombe Technical Community College

Ted Schaefer of Drexel University

Christine Gibbons of John Carroll University

A number of WYNCOM employees also pitched in. We're indebted to Jackson Horton for his striking cover design. Maria Pinczewski-Lee supplied tremendous energy and expertise in helping to manage the many details of production and photography selection that such a book requires. Melissa Fightmaster, Susan Popham, and Shonda Roe, who, along with Debbie Taylor, worked closely with our school partners, gathering all the preliminary information. Tony Condi helped coordinate the printing and overall financing of the book, while B.J. Cobuluis served as coordinator of our publisher relationships and projects. Keith Elkins, Shawnne Dussinger, Chris Tomlin, Maria Pinczewski-Lee, and Robin Roth pitched in as proofreaders— and Lorayne Burns provided an "outside eye" for the final round of proofreading.

We also thank Publications Development Company of Texas for their excellent graphics work on the inside of the book.

Thanks, too, to one of our Lessons in Leadership partners, Dr. Robert Cooper, for his comments on the nature of emotional intelligence, helping us to formulate our ideas on the vital importance of cultivating dreams in order to succeed.

BUNNY AND LARRY HOLMAN
August 1999

PHOTO CREDITS

Most photographs in this book are the personal property of the individual subjects—with the exception of the following: Chapter 2, Willie King in his transmission shop, The Federal Reserve Bank of Atlanta/Flip Chalfant; Willie King head shot, Monsour's Photography, Lake Charles, LA; Chapter 3, Tori Murden closeup, Louisville magazine/John Nation; all other Murden photos courtesy of Sector Sport Watches; Chapter 7, David Lyman photos courtesy of Maine Photographic Workshops; Chapter 11, Juliet Mee photo courtesy of Pat Owens, Springfield, MO; Chapter 14, Jack Canfield photos courtesy of Self-Esteem Seminars, Inc., Santa Barbara, CA.

CONTENTS

Lessons in Leadership from the Ground Up

TURNING
DREAMS
INTO
SUCCESS

1

INTRODUCTION

What is it about dreams that captivates us so? Why do these wispy, sometimes vivid and often mysterious things called dreams strike such a chord in each of us?

Dream. The word itself ranks right up there on the vocabulary hit parade. There are dream teams, dream jobs, dream cars, dreamsicles, dreamboats, dream vacations, dream weavers, dream makers and a thousand other dreamy things that tingle the imagination and move you to . . . well, action.

Not to mention success.

Dreaming is not the first thing you associate with business—or leadership, for that matter. And yet, when it comes to building strong organizations or forging a satisfying career, it's the dream that precedes movement, the dream that ultimately drives you forward and keeps you moving past obstacles and frustrations, straight to accomplishment. If ideas are the intellect's way of finding solutions, dreams are the heart's way of finding success—however you define it.

That's why, when someone says to us, "You're dreaming," we usually smile and say, "Thank you." For some reason, dreams get short shrift in this helter-skelter, everybody-duck-I-gotta-make-a-buck world. But nothing could be more essential to a successful business or a satisfying life than paying attention to your dreams—and acting on the ones that resonate.

As owners of WYNCOM, Inc., we conduct hundreds of Lessons in Leadership® programs each year—featuring some of the most pragmatic, informative and insightful leaders in personal and professional development today. People such as Stephen Covey, Tom Peters, Ken Blanchard and Robert Cooper are at the cutting edge of business and leadership thought, and the sheepskins they bring with them speak to the studied and brilliant ideas they offer.

But each of them is also inspirational, intuitive and imaginative—and for good reason. In today's world, when the foundations of business have been shaken to the very core, the ability to merge practical approaches with the passion of possibility—the magical stuff of dreams—has become essential.

If we weren't forming visions for ourselves and our company, neither we nor our colleagues would be driven to excel. More to the point, we'd run the risk of becoming dinosaurs, stuck in the mud of what worked in the past, oblivious to the new ideas that can make the future secure.

In one of our recent programs, Dr. Cooper, author of *Executive EQ*, made what we think is a telling observation.

"We only use one ten-thousandth of our brain power," he said, "and we only keep one forty-thousandth of our visual field in perfect focus. With practice, by engaging senses with the world, physically our senses can change. Some people see one-fortieth of their visual field. They're the leaders I've observed, and they pay attention like no one else."

Dreams and vision, we firmly believe, are part of that acutely observed visual field. Consequently, contrary to what many people may think, it's the dreamers who are paying the most attention.

In this book, you will meet 13 dreamers—people whose occupations and stations in life are as wide and varied as the dreams all of us harbor. Each of them has turned their dreams into success, and emerged with wisdom that we think you'll find both inspirational and insightful.

But make no mistake: The pursuit of those dreams was not always pretty. Committing to a dream means pulling onto a highway filled with potholes, detours and unexpected hazards. Turning dreams into success is not for the timid, nor is it for those who only daydream. In the doing, what these people learned—about themselves, their organizations, their careers, their values—was every bit as rewarding as the tangible results of success as it's commonly viewed.

We know, because that's how it was for us.

Larry always was, and remains, a dreamer and an adventurer. If he's in New Orleans, he might be meeting with a group intent on putting together a new venture, or he might be trying to find Fats Domino's house (mission accomplished). If he's got one hand on crafting a marketing letter, he's got the other on a military uniform, *a la* General George S. Patton, to give a "speech-to-the-troops" designed to lighten things up with our employees. The one constant has been our dream to have an organization that practices what our speaker partners preach—that you can lead with heart and you can thrive with fun. You can break the rules. You can bust out of the box. And win.

When Larry was a younger man, he once had an interview at a major corporation. Not knowing the kind of aspirations Larry had for himself and others, his prospective employer said, "You know, Larry, if you play your cards right, you could be a vice president here someday." Some cards. Prison sentence, anyone?

We opted for chasing a dream.

In our basement, it turned out.

Sometimes, leadership and success literally come from the ground up. It was in the late 1980s when we first began to act on our dream. And yes, we started out in the basement of our Lexington, Kentucky, home. It had a rough concrete floor. The desk was a door laid across two file cabinets. The washer and dryer hummed right behind the desk, which we suppose simulated a hard drive, seeing how the only word processor we had was Larry's old IBM Selectric typewriter. Actually, we wouldn't wash clothes during business hours because we didn't want people to know exactly where our office was.

From the ground up? From the underground up.

The idea was to put on little seminars. To get people to attend, we wrote marketing letters, called on friends and neighbors to help us stuff envelopes and did all the countless other things it takes to give a dream a recognizable shape. Finally, we hired a secretary. We put her next to the water heater.

Success came in little spurts, and finally we were able to move the office to a second-floor room over a marine supply store. To make an impression—and Larry is nothing if not adept at making impressions—we once persuaded a friend to lend us his office as backdrop for a promotional photo session.

There were a lot of people who called us crazy, but Larry exudes confidence. He turns naysayers into players. Some friends loaned us money. Two of our dearest ones, Arthur and Eleanor Light, worked day and night with us in that musty basement and recruited other envelope stuffers. Arthur would hijack the neighborhood, inviting them over to a "pizza party," handing out postage stamps in the midst of the pepperoni.

You dream big, you act big. As the dream grew larger and we sought bigger venues and a nationwide presence, Arthur and Larry were notorious for their road trips. They'd drive all night. Sometimes they'd find a cheap motel at two o'clock in the morning. An hour and a half later, Larry would be awake and call out Arthur's name. "Are you rested?" he'd ask. And Arthur would get up, hop in the car and they'd be off again.

They'd pop up in, say, Kansas City and call a client, pretending they were in town for another meeting and just wanted to say hello. "As long as you're in town, drop by and talk to us," they'd usually hear. And off Larry would go, trying to make another deal. Once, in New York City, they wound up in the offices of Victor Kiam, the owner of Remington shavers, trying to get him to be a speaker. Kiam invited Larry and Arthur to his Park Avenue penthouse for breakfast, then offered his personal limousine so they could make their other appointments in style. Arthur played chauffeur. Larry played magnate. For years they'd travel anywhere, anytime. To this day, we can safely say that Arthur Light knows the location of every Dairy Queen in America.

Because we didn't have money for plane tickets, we first branched out regionally—holding programs in partnership with schools such as the University of Louisville, Xavier in Cincinnati, Franklin University in Columbus, John Carroll in Cleveland—so we could drive to the events. We invested in a Chevy Suburban and would pile in our "staff." Once, for a program in Detroit, Bunny was driving our personal car, a Lincoln, and got lost in a blizzard on I-75. It got worse. Air was slowly leaking out of the shock absorbers. We brought the car because the program featured one of our first "big name" speakers, Dr. Denis Waitley. By the time we picked him up in Detroit, the car was practically on the ground. We drove to the program through a bad neighborhood, the axles banging on the pavement. When we pulled up to a stop sign, an old woman "flashed" us. If we ever start a Lessons in Laughtership series, she's our headliner.

And so it went. When we finally moved to our current digs, Dudley Square, an historic building that once was a schoolhouse, we felt we had arrived. But the dream was just beginning to take form. From a staff of five, we soon had 90. From there we went to nearly 150. In 1996, we were ranked 32nd on the Inc. 500 list of America's fastest growing privately held companies, and we've made the list every year since.

Our dream was a success.

But there is always a price to pay—one we've paid willingly. Because our business is cyclical and financial institutions don't necessarily understand it (after all, we sell ideas, information and dreams), we've often had to pledge all our personal property to guarantee the next venture. We'd be the first to tell you that it's pretty scary to have everything you've worked for be on the line every single day. But worth it? You bet.

Every dream you chase involves risk. Larry left a comfortable position as a teacher at the University of Kentucky. Bunny was in a job she loved at Transylvania University, working for the school president, heading up her own department, hosting a public affairs television program and working with foreign students. Larry made the leap, and when the business began to look like it might become something big indeed, both of us jumped into the alien world of free fall.

That wasn't easy, because there were tough memories to overcome. When Bunny was still a young girl, her father left his successful job in civil service to try to save his father's failing restaurant. Bunny's dad spent a lot of hours at it. They only had one family vacation in 13 years. Her parents never got away on their own. It was stressful for them, and it was hard on her father. When the business finally went under, Bunny's father called on his friends in government and they helped him back into his old career. But they moved around quite a bit after that. Bunny was the "new girl" in her senior year at a brand new high school, this after having lived in the same town most of her life. So, taking on this new venture was a reminder that risk, indeed, has its dangers.

But, as many of the people in this book will tell you, the toughest times often prove the most rewarding. Bunny learned from her father the value of networking and maintaining your friendships and relationships. She also watched with admiration as he vowed to pay back all the debts incurred by the failed restaurant and worked for years to do it. He couldn't help her in college, so she lived at home for two years, got some scholarships and loans, and worked her way through. She learned self-sufficiency. And she learned that setbacks shouldn't stop you from dreaming.

That's also why we surround ourselves with dreamers at WYNCOM. In building our own success, we've seen a wonderful byproduct: the unexpected delights that result when you give a group of bright and dedicated people the chance to dare and dream themselves.

In December of 1998, both we and the company were featured in a page one *Wall Street Journal* article. In June of 1999, Bunny was named to *Working Woman* magazine's list of the top 500 women owners of businesses. She and other female leaders from WYNCOM attended the "Working Woman 500 Congress: Leadership of the New Millennium." Not bad for a basement beginning.

What's neat about our dream is that it was, in a sense, a case of our separate dreams converging. Bunny has always been a people person, and learned from her father and grandfather—successful as a restaurateur until the problems late in his life—the importance of customer service. Not that they'd necessarily call it that. It came naturally. Bunny used to watch her grandfather, standing at the door in his three-piece suit, beaming his welcome to customers. He truly loved what he was doing.

Both of us share that commitment for pleasing our customers—our speakers, our university partners, our audience and our internal staff. That was a key to our tremendous energy and growth as we acquired partnerships with more than 200 universities in the United States and abroad. But understanding our complementary roles has played a big part.

Larry has been the true visionary for the company from the beginning. He has good instincts and the ability to get others excited about his dreams. That's a talent that too often goes unrecognized. The company reflects his spirit and his enthusiasm, qualities that are vital in today's business environment.

Bunny often downplays her role as that of "the supporting cast." But as a contact person out in the field, bridging distances between people and building those crucial relationships, she in fact plays a lead role. Bringing outstanding programs to areas that don't often have the opportunity to see and hear prominent leadership thinkers in person has been quite rewarding. As a couple, and as an organization, we have been very fortunate.

But that good fortune didn't arrive by pure chance. You make your own breaks. We believe first in the power of dreams, then in working to make them come true. As our good friend

Marjorie Blanchard says, "Response to change and pro-actively managing your life and work is an inside-out job. How often have you noticed the energy level of people who know what they want and what they are willing to give up to get it? The world seems to clear a path for them."

In gathering people together with that kind of energy and drive, we have been able to clear our own collective path. If people come in and voluntarily give their gifts to the job, you've not only got a meaningful environment, but one that will pay for the fulfillment of your people. Our path continues to take us to amazing destinations and even more amazing people.

Following on the heels of our first book, *Lessons in Leadership From Your Neighborhood: Making Connections, Building Relationships, Energizing Communities Where You Work and Live*, this book demonstrates how having a dream is essential to success and strong leadership.

We went looking for people who turned their dreams into success. We wanted to tell their stories, and then talk with them about the difficulties, triumphs and lessons learned. We were not disappointed.

This is a book about people from all levels of life, whether globally well known or living in relative anonymity, whether part of an organization or setting out alone. From this diverse group, we found a consistency of admirable qualities than can serve any of us well. "There are heroes in the seaweed," songwriter Leonard Cohen once penned, and we know what he means.

We found the extraordinary in ordinary people. We found famous people and anonymous people, sharing an almost eerie common bond. We found people who excel because they're committed to a vision, or dream, of something better—for themselves and for the people around them.

We also didn't limit ourselves to traditional ideas of success. The person who has a dream of balancing a career and committing to a quality life—and succeeds in realizing that dream—is as important to us as the individual who has a business plan and becomes CEO of a highly profitable organization. Ideally, in fact, neither of those paths should be mutually exclusive.

Robert Cooper, who continues his pioneering work in the areas of emotional intelligence and excelling under pressure, points out the growing importance of "the human moment in a world vying for our time and attention, and driven by technology that is inadvertently making us invisible and taking away our voice."

Preserving those human moments—in fact, making them the center of our work and focus—is what will keep our organizations fresh and vital, exuding the energy that attracts and keeps great people as employees, partners and customers.

Robert tells a moving story about the depth and meaning of a Tibetan gesture from a little girl in that country. Holding your hands over your heart and saying *tashi deley* means "I honor the greatness in you." The girl wondered if our American "hello" had the same meaning. Robert answered that it didn't, but he wished it did.

We think you'll see the greatness in these 13 people—and recognize in yourself the same greatness that can allow you to dream and succeed. You'll see how you can apply the same lessons they learned. When we give our dreams and the dreams of others our full respect, we honor our own greatness. We give breath to the possible. We fill the sails with hope as each and every dreamer sets a course into uncharted waters.

We've learned countless lessons from this disparate collection of people and personalities. We've discovered that there are as many ways to act on your dreams as there are dreams to be dreamt, that there is no one recipe for professional and personal happiness and success. And we've learned that the best inspiration for thinking big and dreaming bigger is to immerse yourself in a hearty stew of others' ideas and experiences.

That stew is the main course of this book. From leaders in business thought to leaders in governmental agencies, from business to education, and from innovators and entrepreneurs whose names aren't yet as big as their ideas, we'll explore how each of us can turn dreams into success.

Meanwhile, the next time somebody tells you that you're dreaming, just say, "Thank you. Thank you very much."

Willie's World: in the shop; heading up a group of Partners in Manhood kids for an outing; with wife Dorothy and daughters Tamakia, Anita, Mary and Shantall; riding the bull.

2

WILLIE KING

BUSINESS OWNER,
COMMUNITY LEADER

*"Find somebody who wants you to have your dreams.
You've got to search for that true person."*

He remembers the days working under a blistering Louisiana sun, picking cotton. His family barely made enough to eat. He had ideas, but they found no ears. The rest of the family, he says, "just didn't look at life in a progressive manner." So he bought a calf with $16 he'd made to try to start a business, selling it later for a profit. "Just to somehow show them," he says, "that you could process work." He was seven years old.

He remembers the nights hiding behind a Houston garbage can, trying to sleep. He had no money. He stole raisin cakes to survive. And he dreamed anxious dreams—prostitutes on the street coming by every now and then to see if he was OK. "They'd check on me all night long," he says, "to make sure nobody killed me." He was 14.

Willie King remembers—and from each memory a dream for something better emerged. Now, at 45, he's a highly successful owner of several businesses in Lake

Charles, Louisiana. He sits on the board of directors of the local Chamber of Commerce and was named to a regional Federal Reserve Advisory Board. But his dreams reside elsewhere—in the myriad civic groups he either leads or volunteers to work in, the ones that help others, especially children at risk. Willie King remembers those garbage cans.

"The key to progress is people," Willie once told the *Lake Charles American Press*. "If you're there for people, they'll be there for you."

If there's a signature idea that defines Willie's life, it's that. In the worst moments, someone was there to offer encouragement or help. He saw his family of origin dissolve, his first start-up business nearly ruined when his meager set of tools was stolen, and his first thriving business burn to the ground. But always, people were there for him. And always, Willie King worked to keep his dreams alive. Now he's in a position to return the gift.

"Everybody must live his own dream," Willie told *Louisiana Business* magazine—and recalled his own dreams as a child. "I would sit and draw pictures of the house I wanted to have one day on the wall of an old barn." In 1994, he built it, on a seven-acre plot of land.

"When I look back over my life, every time I've seen tragedy it turned out to be a success," he says. "Once I overcame the tragedy, I was a success. And I always enjoyed the challenge."

Among his businesses are King's Transmission Service, King's Funeral Home and King's Meter Reading Service. He's owned many other businesses, including a limousine service, trucking company, real estate firm and financial planning service.

His civic involvement takes on staggering proportions. He's a member of the boards of 14 community service organizations involved in activities such as job training, health services and treatment of substance abuse. He serves as president of Partners in Manhood and the Chenault International Airport Authority. He also works with the Foreman-Reynaud YMCA, the Governor's

Office of Women's Services, the Family and Youth Counseling Agency, the Children's Miracle Network and the St. Patrick's Hospital advisory board. He's chairman of Project Rebuild Future and heads up the local Boy Scouts.

"What is truly amazing," wrote Karen Dawn Wyche-Romero in *Louisiana Business*, "is not merely the number of groups . . . he's involved with, but his commitment to each one."

It's the same commitment he brings to his employees.

"Everyone who works for him truly loves him," says Betty Anderson, acting director of Continuing Education at McNeese State University. "His heart's in the right place. He just has a very astute awareness of how to start a business and help people in the process. When he commits to something, he puts his heart into it."

Talk to Willie a couple of minutes, and that much is obvious. He connects immediately. As he tells his story, he does so with such an engaging mix of passion, laughter and insight that you discover, early on, just why Willie has realized so many dreams and helped so many others realize theirs.

Willie S. King, Jr., is not a chapter. He's a book.

Where to start? Perhaps it's best just to go back to those cotton fields, where Willie would be up before dawn and work into the night—on the small family farm in Washington, Louisiana. But when he was 14 his parents, Margaret and Willie Sr., had a falling out. His father focused his anger on Willie. "My daddy basically put me out," he says. "He told me to leave."

Willie had $10. He spent nine of it for a bus ticket to Houston.

"I'd never been to a city in my life," he says. "But all these folks from the city come down and give you all these wild stories that get you all excited. You think they have the world and you have nothin'. So I spent nine dollars for a bus trip to Houston.

"That left me one dollar. There was this one guy who used to come to the farm, and he was supposed to pick me up. I used the last of my money trying to call him. Well, you know what happened from there. I never got out of the bus station."

He didn't know what to do. "The city," he says, "looked like a monster to me." Forced onto the street, he sought out sanctuary among the garbage cans.

His first break came several days later, when he stumbled upon a veterinary clinic. The owner offered him some money to clean the dog pens. "So I did, probably better than he'd ever seen it, because I made it shine," he says. Before long, the man told him he could sleep inside the clinic. "But he didn't trust me that much," Willie says. "Houston's a big city, and there's a lot of criminals and kids do a lot of crazy stuff. And I understood that."

Eventually, he got a job in the kitchen of a restaurant at Astroworld. He made enough money to buy an old car. He also paid back the place where he'd swiped raisin cakes to survive. Three or four months later, his father found him.

Willie looks back on all this and sees not regrets, but blessings.

"You know, both my mom and dad are great people," he says. "And I wouldn't change a thing that's happened in my life. I've loved it all. When my dad found me, he apologized. Over the years, both he and my mother have gone out of their way to make it up to me, in so many ways."

It shows. Willie is not the only success. Four brothers and a sister have also made their mark in business—although tragedy visited here as well. One of the brothers, Christopher, wound up working in Willie's transmission shop, then moved to Dallas to open his own place. It was thriving until Christopher was killed by a shotgun blast by an unknown assailant. Years earlier, a fifth brother had died in infancy. "Everything happens for a reason," Willie says. "But some things go beyond understanding."

When Willie returned to the farm, he continued to pick cotton and go to school. He'd learned a strong work ethic not only from his father, but also from Joseph Rideaux, the man who encouraged young Willie to buy the calf. It was Joseph Rideaux, in whose cotton fields Willie also worked, who instilled a sense of business possibility. Then, at age 17, Willie married his high school sweetheart, Dorothy Tyler—the start of a family that now includes four daughters.

A stint in the Army followed. He got an associate's degree at St. Martin's University while in the military. When he got out, he moved to Lake Charles and enrolled at McNeese State to continue work on a four-year degree. Willie is the first to tell you that getting a higher education is a plus, but the classroom didn't contain his dreams. He walked out of a class one day, got on his motorcycle and literally rode to his destiny.

"I got on my motorcycle and I knew I wasn't going to go to college anymore," he says. "But I didn't know what I was going to do. I just started riding, just feeling the wind in my hair. And what happened next was, I guess, the key to my whole success financially."

He rode up to an auto shop. Through a big window in the front of the shop, he saw an older man struggling to put an auto transmission onto a table. Willie walked in and helped him.

"And when I touched that transmission," he says, "I knew that's what I was supposed to be doing. I knew that's what I wanted."

He asked the man what time the shop opened the next day. Seven o'clock, the man said. He asked if he could come in to help some more. The man said he had no money to pay him. Willie said that didn't matter. In the dust and grease of the old shop, Willie saw a classroom—and free tuition. He showed up the next morning.

"I went in with my work clothes on because I wanted him to allow me to work," Willie says. "I didn't know a thing about transmissions, but my hands are fast. And I think ahead. Once I saw him grabbing a certain wrench, the next time he needed it I had it sticking out toward him. I learned quickly about cars and transmissions. It's almost as if God gave me the gift.

"I live on maybe three or four hours sleep a night. So I could stay up late and study. If I knew we had a particular kind of transmission to work on the next day, I'd take the manual home with me, and I would study everything there is about that one. Next day I'd come in looking like I knew more than I'd left with."

When the man was later hospitalized, Willie had learned enough to keep the place going. He still wasn't being paid anything. But then came another ironic twist. Another shop had called asking for help with a problem, and Willie had the answer. He went to the other shop and fixed the car for them. Later, when his "employer" found out about it, he angrily told Willie never to do it again.

"Bad move on his part," Willie says. "That was crazy. I would have never done that to somebody. You want to know what happened? I went to work for the other guy and went from zero dollars to $350 a week."

The new job lasted eight months. Willie was doing well, but when the owner's friend returned to town hoping to get his job back as a transmission builder, Willie was the odd man out.

"He told me, 'Willie, you've done a good job and everything, but this guy . . . I've known him for 15 years and he needs a job, and the only one I've got is yours. So I'm going to have to take your job and give it to him,'" Willie says. "So I looked at him and said, 'OK, but, you know, since I've been here your customers really love me. If I'm not here, your business is going to drop.' I tried to sell him on that, but it didn't work."

Willie was fired.

"I told myself," Willie says, "that never again in my life will anybody control whether I feed my kids or not. Never."

Enter Willie Johnson.

Willie Johnson was retired from the railroad. "A few weeks before I was let go, he came by to sell an old transmission," Willie says. "I didn't know him from Adam. We were just chatting back and forth, and for a young guy to come up and talk to him and not talk stupid or foolish . . . he was impressed by that.

"All of a sudden he looked me in the eyes—he's dead now, but I picture him saying this all the time—and says to me, 'I've seen a lot of people in my life, some I liked and some I didn't.' Now, I didn't know where he was going with this. I was a little nervous. And then he said, 'But you, young man, have no business working for anybody other than yourself.' And he gave me his phone number and said, 'If you ever decide to go into business, call me.'"

So when he was fired, he quickly recalled what Willie Johnson had told him. "I remembered what he'd said, and all kinds of things started flashing through my head," Willie says. "I figured this guy had to have a lot of money. This guy's got it going, talking like that."

Turned out, Willie Johnson didn't have any money to loan. He just had encouragement and advice. He told Willie to sell his old camper truck, which Willie did for $500. He spent $250 to rent a little building and most of the rest to turn on the utilities. It was 1979. Willie King was in business. Barely. And Willie Johnson? Did he offer any muscle to the venture?

"Let me tell you what his muscle was," Willie King says, his laugh almost a giggle. "He'd sit down on this white five-gallon can and he'd say, 'Willie, work don't bother me at all. I can sit by it all day long.' He was retired. He wasn't going to do a lick. He said, 'The only thing that I need to be doing here is to make sure that if a car falls on you, I can call somebody to help you out.' He was a great guy. He'd encourage you to go ahead on. And he'd make it a joke. He'd make you laugh even when you were sad."

Business was slow, and when somebody stole all of the transmission shop's tools, it appeared that Willie King's business would die. Willie Johnson came to the rescue, supplying a set of old rusty tools, but Johnson knew that that wasn't the only remedy required. "He told me we needed to pick scrap iron to make some extra money," Willie says, "but that wasn't going to be enough, either. I could ride, though, so I began riding bulls at the rodeo. There was money in that if you won. Between that and picking up aluminum cans, I kept the shop open."

Willie rode bulls more than 300 times. He'd work in the day, ride bulls on the weekends and pick up scrap in between. It was treacherous going to keep the business alive. Then, in the early 1980s, there was a flood. It was Willie's big break.

"One of the reasons I had trouble getting business was because back then, at 25 or 26, I only weighed about 115 pounds and had this little baby face. So people couldn't see me owning a business, in a sense," Willie says. "But when we had the flood there were so many cars with water in the transmissions that the big shops couldn't get to them. Matter of fact, the big shops had so much business that they'd tell people to go to hell in a minute.

"That's when people started searching for unknowns like me. And when they came my way, that was it. They weren't going to go anywhere else after I worked on their cars. I knew that."

The business began to take off. And over the next few years, Willie King's dream turned into a highly rewarding reality. Willie Johnson was there to see it all happen.

"I used to call him Tiger," Willie says, "because he always used to tell me, 'Willie, look, if you're going to make it, you're going to have to fight like a tiger. Don't expect anything simple. Don't expect it free. Don't expect it easy. Just continue to fight like a tiger.'

"Later, I had this belt made for him that said 'Tiger' on it. I always called him Willie Tiger Johnson. In his obituary, they wrote that. Now, I don't know how a tiger fights, but to me it meant don't ever stop, don't ever quit. No matter what happens, you keep on moving. You just keep on moving, keep on fighting, and you'll win."

Later, when Willie Johnson learned he had cancer, Willie King was there for him. "That was when I really got to know the inside of him, when he started telling me the real thing," Willie says. "He'd always wanted a van and he wanted this horse and he wanted to go to Chicago. Before he died, I bought him that van and that horse, and I took him to Chicago.

"The horse was a quarter horse. We named it Tessie. Tiger had always wanted a racehorse. That was his dream, to race this horse. He died before the horse was old enough, but when he got sick, I gave him my word that I'd run this horse for him. After he died, I renamed the horse Run for Tiger. I knew he couldn't race a lick, and I spent a fortune raising and training him—but it was worth it. Willie's horse did get to race.

"I had accomplished so much by the time he died. I had made a lot of money. I had a used car lot then, too. So he could have what he wanted. A lot of people say, 'Well, he didn't give you any money.' No, he gave me more than money.

"You never forget people who help you. I felt as close to Willie Johnson as his own children were. We're still close. Even though he's dead, we're close. You know how people talk about life after death? That man lives in me every single day."

Willie King no doubt calls on the spirit of Willie Johnson as he dreams of leaving a similar legacy for others—and he summons the tiger in Willie Johnson when tragedies strike, like the one in 1993.

"My transmission shop caught fire," Willie says. "I was building a new house, my dream house, and my main source of income burned down. Me and my wife and kids were standing in front of the place, and they were crying. But I just smiled. I said, 'Look, the only thing I see here is an opportunity to put it back together better than what we had before. So maybe we just need to work at putting it back together better.'

"They looked at me like I was nuts. But I had a neighbor, Floyd, and I told him that all we needed was a tractor. We could drag the stuff out, lay down a little concrete and put us up a place on the outside to work. I called the contractor who was building my house and asked him to come out and put up a shed. The fire was on an early Saturday morning. By Monday morning, I was back in business, on the outside. We even built electric lifts and put them in the parking lot so we could raise up the cars to work on them."

He'd work in the transmission shop in the daytime and at night, he and Floyd would haul off the wreckage. He took his motorhome, ran a telephone line to it and used it as the office.

"Insurance companies take forever to pay off," he says, "and we had to stay open to keep the business from going under. It took four or five months to rebuild. We moved back in the building on Christmas Eve. I'm going to tell you another blessing. We worked outside all that time, but we didn't have one cold day. And after we moved back inside? The rest of the winter was cold. Me and my secretary laugh about that all the time. I don't think we even had but one rainy day when we were on the outside."

Place a call to Willie's transmission shop and Jean Fontenot, his secretary, will greet you with the kind of warmth and sense of humor you'd expect of someone who works for Willie King. He met Jean about 17 years ago when she was working as an attendant at a gas station. Willie recognized in her the kind of spirit he admires and offered her a job. They've been great friends ever since.

The challenges, meanwhile, never end. After Willie started a water, gas and electric meter reading service a couple of years ago—something he knew nothing about; he just sat back and delegated the work to others—the manager of the service and all the workers quit *en masse*. "It was like a conspiracy to take the company away from me," Willie says. "They knew how to do it and where all the meters were." Fearing the group would try to strike a deal on their own, Willie temporarily left the transmission business to read meters, learn what it was all about and hire a new workforce. "Now I'm one of the best there is," Willie says. "I can read about a hundred an hour. I'll still go out there and read them to make sure I stay in practice."

All of his children have worked for him, most of them now at the funeral home. All of them have worked at one time or another in the transmission business, too. "I made them get greasy from day one," Willie laughs. "If I got greasy, they got greasy. My oldest daughter knew how to build transmissions. She's a schoolteacher now, but she works with me in the summer."

His wife Dorothy manages the funeral home, often working from 5 A.M. until late at night.

"She's a war-horse, pardner," Willie says. "She can work as hard as I can. I'd always tried to get her involved in one of the businesses, but nothing appealed to her. This didn't either at first, but I practically demanded she try it. I told her that I wanted to find something for her to do, so if something should happen to me she could keep things going.

"She hated the idea at first, but when she saw how she could interact with people in a meaningful way . . . well, if she had to choose now between going to work or staying with me, I think she'd choose going to work."

At that, Willie breaks into laughter again.

He's also very close to his uncle, Raymond King, co-owner of his trucking company. "Raymond has been as close as a brother," Willie says. "He can barely read, but he has this uncanny wisdom, especially when I'm ready to make a mistake. He'll say, 'We need to talk,' and he leads me in the right direction. He's right 99 percent of the time."

One of Willie's latest endeavors is working with Realizing the Dream, an educational venture to help students make career choices. With his own money, he underwrote Teen Summit I, a program which takes on the problem of teen pregnancy. He has another project in mind. "I am going to teach other people to go into business for themselves," he told *Louisiana Business*, "because it's going to be really important over the next few years to know how to be in business for yourself."

And so it goes. Willie King knows no other way. He works because he loves it, helps others because he loves that even more. He's well off financially, a dream fulfilled. More significant, he's discovered this other dream—one of community, where business and social responsibility work hand in hand, where the dreams of one include jump-starting the dreams of others.

A Conversation with Willie King . . .

You've always used the word "can't" as motivation, haven't you.

Always, always—as far back as I can remember. That's because in our community, "can't" was the only thing you ever heard. Anything that looked outside the norm or anyone who looked beyond, they'd say, "You can't do it." If you looked beyond those cotton fields, they'd say, "You can't do it." You can't own a car, you can't have a bank account. All my life I heard that. Even in school. There was one teacher, though, who was very positive. Miss Lydia Lawson. I call her Miss Simmons, because that was her name when she was married for awhile. I still go and see Miss Simmons. She was always the person who said, "You can, you can." She led that "you can" life.

Did you already have that in you, or did she instill it?

I had it in me. I thought you could. But there wasn't anyone who would confirm it other than her and Joseph Rideaux, who was a farmer. Matter of fact, his son Leo works for me today.

Joe was a positive person. He didn't have a high school education, but you could see the dreams in his eyes. Always you could see the dreams. And he could work, too. I admired his work ethic as far back as I could remember. This guy could outwork anybody. He could just go and go and go. And I went to work with him in his cotton fields. I mean, that reinforced what work was.

What was that like, in the fields?

Aww, it was beautiful. But it *was* challenging. You had to get up at 5 o'clock in the morning and not stop until 9 or 10 at night, and in that scorching heat all day long. You'd take an hour for lunch. But we didn't know any different back then. We weren't exposed to all this other stuff—like a 15-minute break in the afternoon and a 15-minute break in the morning. Man, they'd pass down that cotton row with a water bucket and you'd grab a little drink of water and you'd keep on moving—because everybody had goals.

That was one thing about the cotton fields. It was very goal-oriented. I set my goal every day to pick 200 pounds. Two hundred pounds of cotton, that's a lot for a little child. I remember the closest I ever got to my goal was 199, and Joseph Rideaux gave me the other pound.

People like Joseph Rideaux, Lydia Lawson and Willie Johnson helped you reach your dreams. Now that you're a

success, it seems that helping your community and giving people meaningful jobs is as important to you as what you've accomplished in business.

That's *more* important to me than success. A whole lot more. The only reason I think I have financial success is because I can't teach people to do better unless I do it first, you see? You can have all the money in the world. I don't have a problem with money. But if you don't have people to share it with, if you don't have people you love and care about, if you don't have a community that cares about you and that you're involved with, you don't have anything. I don't care how much money you've got; you really are alone and you're lost.

And so, money's good but I think that my community, my people and those youth programs I'm involved in are much, much more important.

Did it take you a while to gain that perspective?

Yes, because initially I thought money was the deal. Initially, I really did. But after I bought the Mercedes and the motorhome . . . I'd take off in the Mercedes, go here and go there, but the Mercedes just didn't fill that gap. It seemed like something was missing. And the motorhome? It was good. But it was a thing. It became work. It became something you looked after.

And then I started getting involved with people. Well, I had always been involved with people, but you lose touch, you lose those little things that were really valuable to you. You just lose them, chasing that dollar bill.

How did you get it back? Did you just begin to realize that something was missing?

Yes. One of the ways I got it back was by working with some younger kids who had nothing. They reminded me of me. One kid in particular who made me make a major turn was a kid named Nathaniel Smith.

What happened?

Well, Nat was in one of the youth programs I worked with—Project Rebuild Future with the YMCA. He was always jolly. Then, all of a sudden one day he was a sad kid. Really, really sad. I'd see him week after week at the program, sitting in a corner kind of by himself and not talking. Before, he used to always be hanging on me and hugging on my waist or whatever.

Although I'd worked with these kids, I never really got into their personal lives because there were like 60 of them and you just tried to keep things in order. But I started talking to Nat and found out that he was basically on the street. His mother was dead and he didn't have contact with his daddy. He lived with his grandmother, who was old and barely could get around.

I took him for a weekend with me, my wife, my daughters and my grandson to a preacher friend of mine. We just spent the weekend out of town and really got to know a lot more about him.

I eventually found that there were people sitting right around me with major problems, and I didn't have a clue. I knew how to make a dollar, but I'm sitting in the midst of a child who I could really help. My head must have been in the wrong place, because I didn't pick it up early. But I did pick it up early enough to get to him in time. Nat's working on the docks now. He's got a family, with a little baby.

And what I found out was that there were a lot of Nathaniels. So I started focusing on young kids. You know, the strangest thing about it is that the more I focused on the community and helping other people, the more money I made. Matter of fact, it's gotten to the point now where, in all honesty, the only thing I have to do *is* work in the community. That's my only job.

I think that God fixed it that way because, even though I go to my business and I try to do some work or find some work, there really isn't any. My people are taking care of it. I want to keep myself involved, but it's hard because they just take care of things.

How have you managed to find people like that? Do you do anything special to build that kind of "can do" workforce?

I think people can be upbeat if you're on a winning team. What I mean by winning team is, even if you're losing you've got somebody on the side who says, "Hey, look, we've been here before. We're going to find a solution. And when it's all said and done, it's going to be OK. We're going to win."

I think that everybody who works for me comes from places where they looked for the boss to be the hard core guy who jumps down your throat and really wants you to give him respect and all that. You understand what I'm saying? When the boss walks in they're supposed to tremble or whatever? I try to bring about a different perspective because I'm not only a boss, I'm a worker, too. I tell them, "Hey, look, it doesn't matter what you have to do. If you need me, call me."

I'll walk in there with a suit, and if they need me to pull a transmission out, I go take the suit off and put a uniform on and pull the transmission out. I wash the parts for them. Sometimes I walk in there and they say, "We didn't have a chance to sweep the shop." I'll go put a uniform on and I'll sweep the shop.

But when I have to be a boss, trust me, I can be that also. I tell them, "Hey, look, I don't mind being your friend. I don't mind being nice. But I'm not stupid and I'm not crazy. We're not going to play games."

You create a climate where people can be their best, but you don't let people take advantage.

By no means, by no means. I've got this crazy kind of smile. And this smile has worked for me for years. When people are telling me something and they expect me to be stupid or think they can get something over on me, I don't say anything. I just smile and I look them dead in the eye with a super beam. I don't say a thing. And they know it didn't work. Before you know it, they'll start to turn things around. You don't have to say a word. That smile. That funny kind of smile. It's not the normal one.

Another person we've talked with, Harold Koning, pointed out that there's a big difference between leadership and boss-ship—that certain bosses want to control everything, but really don't include people or create a feeling of team-work.

They don't. You know, when I look at leadership, I think that the first person you need to learn to lead is yourself. Now that's a difficult challenge. You need to understand that. You need to move. Leadership means moving. Leadership means creative ideas. It means genuine smiles creating that atmosphere. Leadership means you're going to study if you expect somebody else to study. If you want somebody to shake hands and be nice, you're going to do it first. And the people you are leading . . . you need to do it with them before you do it with the customers—because they've got to meet your customers. The customers come after your employees. You've got to lead with them.

Exactly. If you treat people right, then it's going to naturally flow from them to other people—including the customers.

Yes. Not a hundred percent of the time, but most of the time you'll find that. There's some that no matter how nice you treat them, they're not going to be right. But that's the nature of those people.

Sometimes you have to let people like that go. But how much do you try to bring them onto the team first?

You really work with them. You try different techniques. You try walking in there, going to breakfast with them, trying to build that rapport. Because if somebody isn't a team member, that means that they are having some kind of difficulty in their life, because everybody wants to be on a team.

Honestly, everyone wants to be on somebody's team. No one wants to be alone. If they're alone it's because they haven't found out how to fit on someone else's team. And maybe someone didn't have the patience to show them.

Your work with kids and your relationship with employees . . . all of that, in a sense, is creating situations where people can dream. Is that the key?

Dreams? Yes. But I think dreams come after respect. When I work with the kids, I don't try to develop dreams. What I try to develop is respect for themselves and respect for me. You take some of the worst kids out there that everybody says is a bad kid, a deviant kid. I don't have a kid who doesn't call me Mr. King. I mean, it's like that all over the city. I went to the Boys Village, which is kind of like a detention center, and the kids I know over there, holler, "Hey, Mr. King."

And I think that as a black man—and I hate to go into that, OK?—but as a black male, we don't spend enough time reaching back. So many of us have let go of kids out there, or we didn't go back and help the mothers, or help them in some way develop respect. Some of us who are capable, who understand the whole problem, need to go back and help out.

I've heard guys say, "Well, this is not my kid." And I say, "I understand, but it's our community, it's our world, it's our future." And so, just because it's that way and somebody dropped the ball doesn't mean we need to sink the whole ship, you know?

It's getting to be a problem in the white community as well.

Sure it is, but the support system is a lot different. If you take the non-profit organizations and the boards that I'm on, there's a lot more support from the community (for whites) than what we're getting. But we're getting there. It just takes some time. Somebody's got to lead, somebody's got to follow, somebody's got to say it enough times. And you've got to make these outreach programs fun. Make it fun helping children. If you can do enough programs where people see it as an asset to them and a joy to go out there and work with these kids, they're probably going to do it.

You said that you don't really try to build dreams for these kids, but respect instead. Once a person has that, the dreams will take care of themselves?

That's it. That's all you need. If you have respect for yourself and other people, you'll find dreams. And also opportunities. Opportunities are always out there for people if they have respect—because it's a rare thing today for a kid to walk up and be a respectable child and really have manners.

Someone once said that, in looking back on his life, it seemed like a movie to him. He meant that a lot of times he didn't know what was going to happen, but in retrospect, just committing to the "plot" *made* things happen. Opportunities would appear.

You know, it's strange you said that. Last week my wife and I were driving to Atlanta. I'm on the Federal Reserve Bank Advisory Board, and we were going to have dinner with Alan Greenspan. And I told my wife, "You know, who would have ever dreamed this—way back when we were out there in that country field with no shoes on, in dust as high as our knees? But here we are, going to Atlanta to sit with Alan Greenspan."

I mean, some things you never even imagine. But doors open for you.

When I first went on the local Chamber of Commerce, all the black community said, "You don't want to get on that because that's just for white folks." I said, "What?"

And so I joined the Chamber. But the first time I joined it, they literally kicked me off because they had an executive director who was a prejudiced guy. I mean, the first day I was in there he said, "We don't really have anything for you to do." Kinda like pushed me out. But when they got this other guy, Joe Cironi, to lead it a few years later, everything changed.

He asked me to come to the Chamber. I told him no, I'd tried that deal. But finally I said, "OK, but if I get in your Chamber I'm going to work. I'm not just going to be in it." And so Joe and some others said "Yes. Of course!" They were a welcoming group of people.

And that just goes to show you about leadership. The *leader* had changed, not the people. The leader changed and the whole organization changed. And before you knew it, I was on the board of directors of the Chamber of Commerce. And it was from that that I was nominated for the Federal Reserve Advisory Board position.

Let's switch gears. You're known for customer service. You send out birthday cards, you visit with customers and your employees treat customers well. Are you surprised that so many businesses don't understand how important that is?

It's almost like it's a secret, huh?

Exactly. Just common sense would dictate that it's going to help your business.

It is. And it's the only way. Those customers you never lose, because if they've got a problem they'll come back and talk to you because they know that you're their friend. It's crazy not to be that way. But most people cry about business and they advertise forever and spend a fortune on advertising, when all you need to do is go through your customer list. So, every customer who comes to you, regardless of whether they spend two dollars, 10 dollars or whatever it is, you need to get their name, their address, their phone number and their birthday. You don't get the year, because you don't want to embarrass them with the year. You get the month and the date. And you send them a birthday card. And you handwrite it in ink. When you put that ink on it, they know that you took time for them.

And that's not a contrived thing with you, is it. You know how you run into some people saying "Have a nice day" behind a counter and it might as well be a tape recording.

That's crazy, too. They don't even mean it. But no, that's a real thing to me, because it's important for these people to know that I care about them—because without them I couldn't have a business.

How important is trust in leading?

That's major. Your employees need to trust you. A leader needs to be trusted. Your people should never catch you in a lie.

If you had to sum up the secret to turning dreams into success, what would you tell people?

Number one, write it down. Write down what you want.

Number two, you'd better surround yourself with people who want you to have it. That's a major thing for me. Surround yourself with people who genuinely want you to have your dreams, because everybody else wants to take them away from you.

Number three, you've got to commit to them. Either do it or die trying.

And number four, listen to genuine people—because they'll lead you in the right direction.

To get people to want you to have your dream, it's got to be reciprocal, doesn't it? You have to be in tune with what their dreams and wishes are as well.

Yeah, but the only people who are going to want you to have your dream are the people who already have *their* dreams. People who are confident and who are really focused on what they do, they want you to have your dreams. People who didn't get their dreams or aren't moving in the direction to attain their dreams, they don't want you to have yours because they didn't get theirs.

Because your success would remind them of their own failures?

That's right, that's right. So you've got to find somebody who wants you to have your dreams. And that's not easy to find. That's harder to find than it is to build your dreams. But you've got to search for that. You've got to search for that true person.

You're in a position now to be that true person for others.

There are two young men in Houston—Mark and Robert Tigner—I'm working with right now. They called me and they were struggling, saying that they can't get a job, they can't advance. They had so many things they couldn't do, talking about how the whole world was controlled by white folks. They just went on and on and on. And they asked me to come and meet with them in Houston.

Well, I'd had my struggling years, so I went to spend a weekend with them. I sat down at a restaurant in Houston and I listened to them for about an hour. Finally I said, "The only person who doesn't like you is you." They looked at me like I was crazy. They said, "Nobody ever told us *that*." I said, "Hey, man, you all are full of crap. I drove all the way to Houston and I've listened to you, OK? You want to do better?" They said, "Yeah." I said, "No, do you *really* want to do better?" They say, "Yeah." I say, "OK, you do everything I say to do for one year. And if it doesn't work, then I'll come down here and make it work for you. But you've got to do everything I say, read every book I say to read."

You could call these two kids right now. In one year they not only got jobs, but one was the top salesman in his store for eight months in a row, and one went from not having a job to being a customer service manager. And he's also teaching customer service. They've got two brand new trucks. I've got them investing with my stockbroker, and one of them is even dating my oldest daughter.

What books did you suggest to them?

How to Win Friends and Influence People, number one. You've got to read that book every year. That's a must. Number two, *The Magic of Thinking Big.* You've got to begin to focus on your brain power, and begin to think bigger than what you always thought.

And then you go on to read leadership books and sales books and success books—just everything. And listen to tapes. If you don't study those techniques, you cannot win, even if you've got the talent. You have to know how to apply it.

They read over 30 books in one year. And consistently we talked on the telephone. They even cut a CD. They had written music. They had positive music with good musicians, and we cut a CD called "Call Me." Now they're writing music for church, and playing there.

I'm talking about two young men who went from zero to being two of the most excited guys I've seen in my life. They went from having nothing, an old raggedy car that took a gallon of oil a day, to two new trucks, walking around with neckties. When they walk by, people back up from the glare of excitement and expression.

It's funny. When they were complaining to you . . . from their perspective, there might have been an element of truth to the complaints. But the point is, if you focus on that one element, you're focusing on the negative, and what else are you going to get but negative?

That's it. I focused on the other. And I made them a promise: "It's impossible for you to fail." And literally it is. It's impossible for a black man to fail. Can you imagine a young black guy walking up with a tie, saying "Yes sir, no sir" with positive information and no negative orientation? Can you imagine what it was like when one of those guys walked up? That charisma was just boiling out!

And many of these kids don't see that. I told them, "Man, look! Look at all your friends. I want you to do just the opposite.

You have the advantage. You don't have any competition. Your competition is you. Number one, you're young, you're black, you've got information everybody else is unfamiliar with—not to mention I'm your support system. I won't lead you wrong. Trust me."

And they took off, pardner. And let me tell you something, they not only took off, they are *flying* by. I talked to them the other night. They're going to pass me up like a jet. They will.

This has got to be as rewarding a dream as you could ever want.

Oh, it's a whole new game. Just like I tell the stories about Joseph Rideaux and Willie Johnson and how they helped me? Well, now these kids have written a song about me. That made me feel so good. That made me feel better than all the money in my life. They mention in the song all the things that we went through that year.

What do you think stops a lot of people from going after their dreams?

Fear. They're scared. And you want to know what? I'm scared, too! I am! To tell you the truth, I'm just as scared as everybody else. But I know one thing. If I go at it, I'm going to find a way to win. I think my fear comes when I don't know how much it's going to take out of me to win, because I know I won't quit until I win. I'm either going to do it or die trying. So there's that scary part where I put my life on the line for what I want. That's non-stop.

But when you mention fear, you laugh.

Yeah [he laughs again]. Fear is so devastating and it can drain so much energy out of you. Even something as simple as public speaking. Can you imagine how devastating it is to a lot of people just to walk in front of that crowd? And you know they're not going to do anything. They're not going to shoot you! They're not going to laugh at you or criticize you. They're going to give you encouraging comments even if you did a lousy job.

But the fear to walk in front of people . . . whoo, it kills a lot of people. It almost killed me. But I had to challenge it. Once I found out I had a fear that bad, I challenged it. And four months later I was competing in the national finals in Fort Lauderdale, Florida.

In what?

In public speaking. Toastmasters.

Really?

Sure, but I was so scared the first time I spoke. It was at the opening of the funeral home, and the man I'd hired to speak couldn't make it—so I was stuck having to do it. I had to get in front of these people and my shoes were wet. Sweat was running down my pants leg. I knew I had to do this little speech. It wasn't but a five- or six-minute speech. But my brain was going away. I was going crazy. I didn't know what to do. And so, I recognized right then that you cannot live that scared. You cannot live a life where if you try to give a talk, it kills you.

So how'd you get through it? Did you just say "I'm going to do it anyway"?

Yeah. I had to do it because I had too many people looking at me. The mayor was standing there, and the president of the Chamber of Commerce was standing there.

But not long after that, I won the Toastmasters local competition and the district. Then they had a competition in Fort Lauderdale where they pay you to go and you compete against 12 or so finalists.

I overcame that fear. And since then I've done hundreds and hundreds of speeches. Now it's just like walking up to turn on my TV. I'm still somewhat nervous, but I'm nervous because I want to do a better job, always a better job.

Well, it's almost like the "can't" thing you were talking about. You feed off it and turn it into a positive.

That's right. It's motivation. It's a "can't." Just tell me I can't do it, and I'll prove you wrong.

So many people tell us that fear can be the biggest enemy.

Fear is my buddy. It has always been my buddy. It just brings out the best in you.

Problems bring out your best, too.

Yes. If you got up every day and you didn't have any problems, what are you good for? What would you do if everything was always perfect, everything was always all right? Problems. You've got to have some problems to work on and grow from. I love 'em, I love 'em.

Tori Murden: as at home rowing the Atlantic as she is in helping neighborhoods thrive and the Muhammad Ali Center in Louisville become a reality.

3

TORI MURDEN

ADVENTURER, SEARCHER,
PUBLIC SERVANT

"I want to steal fire from heaven and
share it with the world."

Some people's personalities defy category, blending Type
A frenzy with a simple calm, a quest for answers and solutions with an appreciation for good fortune and the mystery and allure of adventure. Rather than try to label
them, we learn instead just to enjoy their next move,
wherever it might lead.

Such is the spirit of Victoria Murden, called Tori by
virtually everyone, including the thousands around the
world who followed her attempt to row her specially designed vessel, *American Pearl*, 3,500 miles across the
Atlantic alone and unsupported during the summer of
1998. Unfortunately, the furious remnants of Hurricane
Danielle caught up with her, forcing an emergency rescue through the combined efforts of the British Royal
Air Force and a cargo vessel aptly christened *The Independent Spirit.*

"I felt like I went 12 rounds with Mike Tyson," she
said immediately after the rescue. "I was knocked around

37

quite a bit. I tore a rotator cuff in my right shoulder, but it will heal. During the last capsize before I decided to end the row, I was pitch poled. The boat went end over end. The sea anchor was tangled over the bow. I was convinced I would die."

While labels can't do her justice, challenges perhaps best define Tori Murden. What's remarkable is the wide range of those challenges—whether she is taking on the Atlantic alone, or serving as an administrator for the city of Louisville, or engaging in countless other pursuits that, woven together, create a rich tapestry of both personal adventure and public service.

Tori is all about discovery—not only of what the world has to offer, but of what she can learn about herself.

"The best thing to come out of the Atlantic trip and 85 days alone is the feeling that the inside matches the outside," she says. "I want to hold onto that as long as possible. The healthy side of that solitude is recognizing that we're all on a journey. Some of us are here, some of us are there."

As one who dreams big, Tori is at home with change, flexible enough to adjust to unexpected obstacles, open enough to welcome a diversity to her dreams. Tori doesn't believe in limiting herself, or the scope of her vision. She doesn't just dream big, she dreams wide. Hers is a world rich in possibilities. More important, hers is a dream that includes encouraging others to realize their own dreams.

"When I talk to teenagers about it, my favorite speech is called 'Shakespeare, Quantum Physics and You,'" Tori says. The gist of it is 'Don't pigeonhole yourself. Don't choose a path and stick to it at the cost of everything else.' I describe my forays into pre-med, divinity and law schools not as taking different paths, but going in a straight line over different terrain."

Tori ended her row just five weeks and 950 nautical miles from Brest, France. Over 85 days she rowed more than 2,600 nautical miles, most of those days utterly alone, after her communications via e-mail were knocked out early in the journey.

"I lost contact with my Gulf Stream analyst, who could tell me where this really fast river running through the ocean was going," she says. "I went from covering 80 to 100 miles a day to sometimes going backwards. That was a result of being out of communication.

"The hard part was the same sort of difficulty I had in Antarctica: getting up in the morning, expending energy all day, and pitching camp in a spot that looks just like the spot you just left. It doesn't change."

Along the way, however, she also experienced the euphoria that solitude in the natural world can bring. Rather than being lost at sea, she was, in a sense, found there.

"I think I had some of the happiest days of my life out on the ocean," she says. "The whales within inches of my boat, the dolphins, the sunrises, the sunsets . . . I felt as if I was holding life in my fingertips, feeling what it's really like to be alive on this planet."

Taking on an entire ocean by herself was just the latest in a young lifetime of adventures for Tori, who is 35. She was the youngest member of the International South Pole Overland Expedition, cross-country skiing 750 miles across Antarctica to the geographic South Pole and thus becoming one of the first two women to ever ski to that point. She's also climbed mountains all over the world, from Alaska to Bolivia to Kenya. She's kayaked in Prince William Sound and the Indian Ocean, and contended for a single sculler position with the 1992 U.S. Olympic Team.

She is an athlete of ideas as well. Since earning her undergraduate degree at Smith College in 1985, she has received a masters of divinity at Harvard and a law degree at the University of Louisville. She has worked as a hospital chaplain in inner-city Boston, and as an administrator for programs to help the homeless. In Louisville, she has served as the project coordinator for public policy, Office of the Mayor, where she helped to create the Community Development Bank and CityWork—an award-winning program designed to revitalize the productivity of the municipal government, modeled after GE's Work Out program. She also fought for the unilateral declaration of a disenfranchised area of the city as an Empowerment Zone, helping to raise almost $70 million to revitalize the community.

Tired yet? Most of us would be. But like the world-class athlete she is, Tori finds that extra burst of energy by feeding off the flow of the action. Rowers (and musicians too, for that matter) call it "the swing"—that ideal blend of rhythm and power that catapults you magically forward. One leap brings on another, and dreams arise from other dreams, seemingly of their own accord.

But behind the eye that envisions is the back that carries the load. And pulling your vessel out of a desperate situation takes gritty effort and hard work.

For five years, Tori navigated a choppy economy and roiling crime as project administrator for Empowerment Zone initiatives for the Louisville Development Authority. In her group work and her solitary achievements, she has found crosscurrents that motivate, educate and humble her.

"If any group understands my disappointment at not finishing the row, it's that community," she says of the neighborhoods she worked with. "They're more alone at sea than I ever was. I was out there with a heck of a lot of resources at my disposal, and they don't have the same recourse. They can't push a button and have someone come in and rescue them."

Since their inception, Empowerment Zones have been criticized in some quarters for being exactly the opposite. But if ever the "E"-word were in authentic practice, it would be in the communities of Louisville's West End: Smoketown, Shelby Park and Phoenix Hill.

"The whole gist of the Empowerment Zone process is to get grassroots communities fired up about what they can do in their neighborhoods," Tori says. "It's not what I would do as a policy wonk, it's what *they* want to do.

"The residents were very clear: 'We don't need social services. We're tired of it. Give us access to capital, give us access to credit and to jobs. By creating more small businesses, we'll create more jobs, which means fewer people on the welfare rolls.'

"We were diligent about giving them what they asked for. We created a Community Development Bank which has been far exceeding expectations. They've created deals we didn't even imagine were out there."

Thus a servant leader has brought new energy and direction to a chaotic situation, helping the disenfranchised pursue their dreams with a renewed sense of purpose.

"It's created a sense of possibility that wasn't there before," Tori says. "I don't think as a public servant you can do much better than that, helping to bring about that sense of ownership in a neighborhood that says 'We can make this place better.'"

The American need for heroes can be almost as worrisome as it is genuine. From jocks to movie stars, country singers to pop psychology gurus, the hero circuit attracts what some would call an inordinate share of money, fame and worshipful energy. Tori Murden has experienced her share of it since her return, making appearances on *The Discovery Channel* and *The Rosie O'Donnell Show*, tasting the strange brew of celebrity hype mixed with the realities of true life-and-death situations she's encountered.

"That circuit is more difficult—it's certainly more challenging emotionally, to remain genuine and true in the midst of the storm," she says.

So how can you inspire people to bring that sense of gung ho energy and cheerleading into their own lives?

"One thing I got out of the trip is that drive that makes it possible to 'keep on keeping on'—the ability to reduce life down to the elements," she says, "to get rid of the superfluous stuff that goes along with a materialistic agenda or an agenda of power. I have just as many agendas as anybody else, and that kind of adventure helps me sort those out.

"Since I've been back, there's been a real shift in my speaking. I used to write speeches for a standing ovation—I knew what it took, and it was a game. It wasn't about making a genuine connection with the audience, it was about making them love me. Now it's not about that at all. It's more about convincing them that I'm no different from them. There are folks who are so far ahead of me I can't believe it. Whatever group it is, there's something positive that I find and point out to them, saying 'This is what you do well.'

"I spoke to Brown-Forman (one of the largest American-owned companies in the wine and spirits business) recently, and they're one of the finest corporate citizens in Louisville. You walk into any shelter or arts event, and there's Brown-Forman money in most of the positive things in this community. There are people like Milton Friedman who say there's no such thing as corporate citizenship, that the only duty of a corporation is to maximize profit. But here's a corporation that clearly doesn't follow that mold, and makes a big difference to the community . . . the community would be diminished if they weren't a part of it. It's time to give them the ovation.

"Even beyond what the organization does, there's a call to good citizenship as human beings living with other human beings, and we can't ignore each other's pain. That's what it's all about."

It's fostering that sense of genuine connection that drives Tori to greater heights, as if her adventures were indeed the stuff of heroic legend. Only she wants the myth brought back down to earth.

"I believe we're all capable of living up to large," she says. "We all have opportunities every day to exercise that. Getting people to not only hear it, but to feel it and believe it, is a really exciting challenge."

As she said in a Louisville *Courier-Journal* profile by Linda Stahl, "You have to chase your dreams. If there is anything I want people to take away, it's that."

As dreams go, there's nothing quite like the recurring kind.

In 1997, Tori and partner Louise Graff attempted to be the first American, and first female, duo to row across the Atlantic, east to west, during the Great Atlantic Rowing Race.

The race was a nightmare, one huge obstacle after another. There were problems clearing the boat through customs in Africa, then a hole in the hull caused by clumsy dockside handling. Even before the race began, Tori's stomach was queasy. It turned out to be more than nerves. She had a severe case of food poisoning. Graff heroically rowed her back toward shore and rescue. They even tried again a few days later—"I still wanted to do it because of all these nuns from Eastern Kentucky and grandmothers and other folks giving us $25 checks," Tori says— but this time the electrical system failed. At least this nightmare had a quiet ending, and Tori immediately set her sights on her next waking dream, the west-to-east solo trip.

After surviving hurricanes Bonnie and Danielle during that subsequent attempt, however, you might think Tori would be ready to ply the relatively placid waters of the Ohio River for a while. You'd have to think again.

"Last October, when Louise Graff and I stepped off the plane that brought us home from the Canary Islands, I carried in my hand an American flag," wrote Tori to her supporters after her solo rescue. "I carried in my heart the dream of returning to the Atlantic to finish what we'd started. In the airport, I promised friends and reporters that the dream was not dead and that the American flag would fly once more over the *American Pearl*."

After being given up as lost at sea, her vessel was rescued 40 miles off the coast of Portugal by the oil tanker S.R. Mediterranean. It temporarily resided in Le Havre, France, then was delivered to Louisville in spring 1999 by a large UPS cargo plane.

With a Norwegian woman scheduled to make a crossing in fall 1999, Tori's schedule was bumped up to the same time period by her sponsors, Sector Sport Watches. Being first, after all, is what counts the most to them. The change in schedule will allow her to attempt the "easier" southern route again, alone this time, traveling with the trade winds from Easter Island to the Caribbean.

"I have learned that there is no such thing as failure," she says, "only the failure to try again."

There's something inevitable about big dreamers connecting.

Through Tori Murden's exploits, her loved ones, colleagues and thousands of followers learn a little bit more about her and about themselves. The website following her daily progress when she attempted her solo Atlantic row attracted over 68,000 visitors from 20 countries.

As her time working for Louisville Mayor Jerry Abramson drew to a close along with his term limit, Tori pondered her future. As she is fond of saying, the dream remains the same—its shape just changes.

"I could go to Washington, I could go sell solar panels in the Third World," she said at the time. "I'm waiting for that still small sledgehammer to let me know what's next."

Or maybe it was that still, small left jab.

"*Dear Tori,*" began one of those many e-mail messages on her website, "*From one Louisville native to another, I wish you the best of luck on your journey across the ocean. We are cheering for you! You are a champion. Best wishes, Muhammad Ali.*"

It should not surprise you that, today, Tori finds herself working as development director for the fledgling Muhammad Ali Center, an exciting new project being constructed in the heart of downtown Louisville. Part museum and part community center, the institution will provide a sense of Muhammad Ali's incredible life journey and will explore the themes of that life: his message of tolerance and healing, of pride and empowerment, of health and dedication, of athleticism and spiritual centering.

"The Center will not only celebrate the remarkable life of Muhammad Ali," Tori says, "but will also demonstrate the catalytic impact that his actions have had on some of the most important social issues and distinguished people of the last three decades. It will explore his boxing career and his involvement in the political, social and humanitarian issues of our times."

And just as her rowing and mountaineering adventures have not been all about her, Tori looks for this new site to be about a lot more than one man, however wonderful he may be.

"The Center will be organized to weave Muhammad Ali's personal story with broader, more universal themes," she says. "His life story will act as the spine of the exhibition, while themed areas will take an in-depth look at topics such as health and wellness, conflict resolution and tolerance."

In weaving her own story and chasing her own dreams, Tori's devotion to cultivating tolerance has deep roots.

"My drive to work with marginalized populations stems from my having grown up with a mentally retarded brother, Lamar," she says. "We moved 13 times. It is hard enough to be the new kid on the block, but to be a new kid on the block with a handicap is a profoundly difficult task. The world of childhood takes on ugly hues when viewed from this perspective. Life is not only 'not fair'—it is not kind and not pleasant."

So she became the ultimate big sister, going beyond example-setting and mentoring to the literal guardianship of her brother.

"My initial ambitions were quixotic," she explains, invoking yet another dreamer's name. "I wanted to make the world 'safe for democracy' or at least safe for my brother, Lamar. Some part of me still does. In my article for *Louisville Magazine* I wrote about 'Promethean ambitions': my desire to steal fire from heaven and to share it with the world. I still think this is possible."

At the Ali Center, Tori's hope is that visitors will gain a deeper understanding of the life and times of "The Greatest," and that their visit will empower them to achieve their highest aspirations.

That's a big vision. But there's precious little doubt in the air when big dreamers come together.

A CONVERSATION WITH TORI MURDEN . . .

What does this position with the Muhammad Ali Center mean to you?

Philosophically, there's a nice overlap. My project and the Center are both about chasing dreams, and doing what it takes to achieve those dreams.

My big concern is the educational focus. How do you go from a skinny 12-year-old to Olympic champion? What does it take to make that sort of progress? If you want to do that same sort of thing, you have to eat, sleep and train right. There will be a gallery about civil rights, showing how Muhammad and others address those issues. Further on, his work on hunger, tolerance, healing, almost a spiritual side. He is a Muslim but doesn't want to focus on religion, unless it's a faith-based discussion of how to lead a thoughtful life.

The Muhammad Ali Institute will focus on conflict resolution, and more academic pursuits, somewhat like the Carter Center. We are in partnership with the University of Louisville in the areas of mediation and conflict resolution. That may be anything from domestic violence to the Dayton Accords. Heads of nations will come, because Muhammad Ali will say, "Come. Talk." When Ali wants to meet with you, access is usually not a problem."

We're in a unique position in that people will come for any number of reasons. When you have the canvas of Ali's life to work with, there's a lot of room to run around. The hard part is maintaining focus. So Lonnie (Ali's wife) and Muhammad are asking, "What will people take away, what will touch them?" We're trying to answer those questions right now.

As someone who has not only realized his dreams but awakened that possibility in countless others, Muhammad Ali seems to have a special sort of magnetism. What do you see in him?

I see this magical spirit when I see Muhammad. Old men will come up and hug him. Mothers will put their babies in his arms. Everyone feels they have access to him, and the reality is they do.

Watching some of those early films, you can see he was grandstanding, saying stuff just to be outrageous. He didn't always have the sense of peace he projects now, that sense of real genuine goodness. You see that there was something special there, but you see that he's grown into this world ambassador that he's become. The neatest thing is to watch him with children, who have absolutely no concept of who this man is, no idea he was the world champion. They just turn and run to-ward him.

A similar connection seems to exist between you and your brother Lamar. How has he fueled your quests and in-spired you?

I have two brothers, one older brother who has multiple sclerosis, who's doing well right now, and one, Lamar, who is mentally handicapped. It's harsh. We moved a lot of times, so for him to always be the new kid on the block, and having an impairment, was pretty horrific. I've seen firsthand how mean people can be. It's that fear factor, that ignorance.

Watching kids being mean to Lamar had less to do with him being a threat and more to do with them not knowing that retardation isn't contagious. As you're growing up, you're so busy trying to define who it is you are, you pick on those things that are "other." The less secure you are, the more you need to point to that other thing.

My mind just made a jump to 1992, when I went to the na-tional training camp to train for the Olympics. I met a lot of folks who were really mean and nasty to me. Looking back, I see that the ones who were nice were the really good athletes, the ones who were secure, who were not threatened by yet another six-foot-tall woman who was really strong. But those who were on the edge, with that fear of the unknown about making the team, were real jerks.

I've thought a lot about that in watching Muhammad, and people who are secure in their jobs and secure within them-selves. They're genuinely nice folks, because they know who they are, they know where they're going and they're not con-cerned with who's stealing their candy.

Look at Muhammad and the impact he's had on civil rights. He marched around the world in 1963 shouting "I am the greatest," and nobody could prove him wrong. For an African-American to do that was unheard of. Then he refused to step forward for the Vietnam draft and was excoriated. He said,

"I'm not going to go shoot a bunch of folks who never did anything to me, to defend a nation where I can't go buy a hamburger at a restaurant because of my skin." They stripped him of everything he had: his title, his ability to box. They threatened him with a five-year sentence. He didn't flee to Canada. He didn't run away. He stood right here and said, "I'm not going." Actually, being Muhammad, he said, "You can put me in front of a firing squad and I'm not going to do it." That meant a lot to people watching him.

He was the only person who went through three levels of counseling to have his CO (conscientious objector) status questioned. Every counselor said he should be given that status, and the draft board kept saying "no" despite those recommendations. I'm absolutely sure it had to do with the fact that he was black and well known. They were afraid that if Muhammad Ali didn't step forward for the draft, there would be all sorts of other African-Americans not stepping forward either. If you look at that war, the kill ratio of blacks to whites is pretty darn high.

I've found that if you bump into something that isn't fair, fix it if you can, and if you can't, don't waste a lot of energy on it. But most things are fixable. I always think of something Andrew Jackson said: "One person with conviction makes a majority."

What were some people's initial reactions to your dreams? Who doubted them, who supported them?

The world needs dreamers. I have been fortunate. My dreams are realizable. They may not be easy, but they are achievable. The work to improve neighborhoods progresses one step at a time: one person, one house, one block and one street. It's a bit like trying to row across the North Atlantic. One cannot imagine the few million strokes needed to cross an ocean. So, one focuses on the next stroke, the one after that and the one after that. Before long a thousand miles have gone by.

What threatens most dreams is a lack of resources. Columbus had to raise money, as did Robert Scott, Edmund Hillary, Charles Lindbergh and most other explorers. Social reformers always struggle for the charitable dollar. The more admirable the dream and the more talented the dreamer, the less difficulty there will be in finding the resources. For me, resource acquisition is the most difficult part of pursuing any ambition.

What have you given up to pursue your dreams? How difficult has it been to do so?

Dreams take time. Training to chase the dream takes time. Rowing oceans and working with marginalized populations are not highly compensated endeavors. I've set four world records, attained three world firsts, academically I have two terminal degrees, and I drive a Geo Metro.

How did you adjust your dream to reality? How did the dream you realized differ from your initial dream?

Hurricanes happen on the ocean. Hurricanes happen in politics. Hurricanes happen within cities. One cannot guarantee success, but, as has been said, "One may ensure that one deserves it."

The dream hasn't changed. The shape of the dream changes as I pursue it over different terrain, but the dream is the same.

Traversing that terrain sometimes requires a guide. You have said it would take hours to talk about all the mentors who have provided you guidance. So describe just one mentor who has strongly influenced you in your work and in your life.

I had a history teacher in high school named Helen Longley. She saved my life. I could have gone off the deep end. She recognized something in me that she wanted to spur on. Like most teenagers I had things going on at home that I really wished weren't going on. She said, "Get on with it. We'd all like to curl up in a hole sometimes and wish it would all go away. You have too much going on, too much talent to waste it."

So she basically kicked me in the seat of the pants when I needed a kick. Kids ask me, "Who did you look up to when you were our age?" When I say teachers, they react with horror. But I say, "You're going to look back some day and realize there's some teacher here now that made a big difference in your life." "No way," they say. I look back at my yearbook and we all made comments like "Man, I hate this place," or "I can't wait 'til I'm outta here," but now I look back on collegiate prep life as a haven. It really transformed my character.

And you have obviously helped to transform other lives in your turn. How do you work to help others pursue their dreams?

I am only now beginning to realize the inspirational character of an individual with conviction. Yesterday, a young man I coached for several years telephoned from Georgetown University to tell me that his crew had won the Big East rowing championship. He just wanted me to know. The dream is not always about achieving things, but about the opportunities one can create for others.

I spend a good deal of time traveling to schools and speaking with young people. I am honest in that I don't consider myself all that special. I tell them that there is more to being a human being than what one owns and what one earns, and that there are higher goals than the pursuit of personal luxury. I regularly receive notes from children about something I said and what it meant to them.

When have you found direction or inspiration from an unexpected source?

Every time I've doubted myself or my ability to survive (literally) a particular hazard, I've found inspiration from unexpected sources. Homeless people, drug dealers, juvenile offenders, dolphins and stars have all inspired me at one time or another. This says nothing of how inspiring the presence of wild creatures can be to a person who is afraid of being eaten.

How do you set aside time and energy from the everyday management of details to devote to the visionary leadership work that keeps you energized and charting new courses?

When in doubt, row. Exercise time is thinking time for me. Time to meditate, time to listen, at bottom the time to pray is all rolled into a socially acceptable activity like rowing, bicycling or roller-skiing.

What tools do you use to overcome fear of action or "analysis paralysis"?

I don't suffer from that problem. I have the opposite difficulty. I take action and apologize for mistakes. I take seriously the old adage that one will not be judged by the choices one made, as much as by the choices one did not make. I seldom regret the things I do so much as the things I do not do. As Martin Luther suggested, "If one must sin, sin boldly."

Sometimes actions come into conflict. How do you turn situations of conflict or struggle into productive solutions and positive outcomes?

The first step is to not run away. This lesson was taught to me when I worked with terminally ill people. Often there was a tendency as the illness progressed for the dying individual to drive others away. It was sometimes their last exercise of control. They'd rather drive someone off than to have them walk away out of fear or repugnance. I learned that if I could weather the storm the relationship would be stronger. If I was lucky, I could share in the last moments of life. Because of this, I was able to experience magical moments. Not everyone is lucid at the end, but when you encounter an intelligent person facing the ultimate unknown, they are often eager to lend expression to the wonder.

The same is true with other conflicts. I think one serious hazard in our time is a fear of anger. Instead of expressing feelings of distress or outrage, we evade it. The anger builds until there are gunshots and explosions. This is a sign that people feel they are powerless to change the shape of their worlds short of cataclysm.

You have always emphasized your love for this country, and even celebrated the Fourth of July during your Atlantic row with sparklers and a solo rendition of the "Star Spangled Banner." But that doesn't seem to be a broadly shared sentiment these days. Is patriotism a dream?

Being an American is a glass half empty or half full. If you really focus on it, the things that bind most cultures don't bind us. We have no common ethnic or religious or historical views. So the things that tie us together are esoteric: the belief in the Declaration and the Constitution. Things that we can debate screaming red-faced. "Are we really all created equal?" "Are we here to promote the general welfare?"

To me, the sense of being part of what is probably the greatest nation on earth at this time binds us together in a sense of privilege. Most of the poorest folks in this country are better off than pretty OK people elsewhere. At some gut level, we understand that. I'm pretty darn proud to be an American. So patriotism is a dream, but it's a good one to have.

For some of those whose glass is half empty, things just never seem to be fair. When things aren't fair, how do you hang on to dreams? How level can we make the playing field, and when do we decide to go find another field?

Mountaineering reminds me of the importance of the human equation. In the back country, ability and need find a balance: to each, according to her needs; from each, according to her ability. In this expedition equation, the superior becomes the servant of all. One who *can* carry more *does* carry more.

I know from mountaineering that summits are sweeter if every member of the team makes it to the top. For me, this ethic transfers to the civilized world. John F. Kennedy once said: "This will not be a great country for any of us to live in if it is not a reasonably good country for all of us to live in."

In the expedition paradigm, if the poor or the ignorant or the weak are slowing our progress toward a higher plain (or higher plane) we must assist their climb by clearing a trail. Ignoring their difficulties will only leave them incapacitated by poverty, ignorance and despair. Wait too long and they will be truly disabled and all of society will be forced to carry their dead weight.

In the back country, the playing field gets leveled, because the superior becomes that servant. The person who's physically or intellectually weaker gets the care he needs. In "civilized" society, we're not always so good about that—"I'm big and strong and I'm going to make as much money as I can and to heck with the rest of the world." Through the passing generations, we're creating poverty and despair and pain and suffering. It leads to things like Littleton, where it sounds like you had a group of kids who felt they had special entitlement to pick on other kids, and finally those other kids retaliated in the only way they thought they'd be successful, which was all-out war. If at some point they'd all been stuck on a mountain together, they might have all figured out how to get along.

Clearly there are a lot of wonderful people in the world who realize there's more to life than the pursuit of personal luxury. But we tend to idolize beautiful, lucky, wealthy people who aren't necessarily those who give back to the ones who aren't so beautiful and lucky. As I set out on another adventure, I recognize I've been pretty darn lucky as I've gone through my life. Overall, I'm one of the fortunate few who has been able to do what she wants and get away with it. So I do feel that sense of responsibility, to young people in particular.

That's something that brought me to the Muhammad Ali Center. Muhammad's whole life since boxing has been about giving back. He has given away more fortunes than you or I will ever see, and that's pretty special. There are lessons in his life that should be perpetuated.

Your discussion of mountaineering brings to mind an ethi-cal parable making the rounds in business circles. A group has trained for a long time for a Himalayan expedition. They are nearing the summit, using every ounce of energy at their disposal, when they meet a Himalayan holy man—a sadhu. He's not in very good shape. He's on a spiritual mis-sion, but he might also die. Should you abandon your mis-sion and intervene for his welfare, or leave him to his choice and fate?

I think you leave him alone. It's different. I've literally been on a mountain where an older German fellow was clearly suffer-ing from high altitude cerebral edema. He was in bad, bad shape. We got him off the mountain, and that was without ques-tion what we should have done. Because he wasn't there for some spiritual purpose, it wasn't a conscious choice to go up the mountain and die. When you're dealing with a religious person on a pilgrimage, he might well be just fine. Out on the Atlantic or up on the mountain, I might be having the time of my life, but I look like hell.

When I was skiing to the South Pole, frostbite on my face, hands cracked and bleeding, I saw this cloud formation over the surface of the snow and the sun was just right, everything was green and purple and incredibly majestic, and I thought, "This is where I'm supposed to be." If my best friends had seen me at that moment, they would have said, "Oh my God, let's get her out of here." I didn't look so good, but I felt OK.

In the middle of the hurricane, I made a conscious decision not to set off the EPIRB [Emergency Position Indicating Radio Beacon]. I chose to put myself out there on a rowboat. That's very different from a fisherman or sailor or steamer captain on a necessary and proper purpose. If I were catching tuna for a liv-ing, of course I'd set it off. But to ask someone to rescue me is going over the line. I don't know if that puts me on the spiritual side of the mountaintop rescue equation, but there was some-thing different about my endeavor that meant it wasn't right to ask other people to risk their lives to rescue me.

As long as we're talking about moments of truth, describe a point in your life when you changed in a major way—a turning point.

Every time I return from a major journey, I find myself changed. My favorite hobby is high-altitude mountaineering. Lugging ice axes around is a strange pastime for a woman from Kentucky, but mountaineering gives me an excuse to journey into simplicity. In the mountains I rediscover how little I can get by with and not how much. In the back country, I sort out the superfluous from the necessary. With this shedding, my intellectual and emotional loads lighten and I return ready and able to tackle the grand and more challenging adventures of the workaday world.

Those adventures only seem to escalate and multiply in your life. What's your dream today?

I want to raise enough money to build another boat and go back to the Atlantic. I want to build the Muhammad Ali Center. I want to steal fire from heaven and share it with the world.

Steve Lambert anchors his dreams by asking the right questions and being willing to adapt.

4

STEVE LAMBERT
SMALL BUSINESS
OWNER, ENTREPRENEUR

"The big enemy is a steady paycheck."

Can dreams turn into chain reactions, with one triggering another and another and another? It would seem so in the case of Steve Lambert, owner of Aim Electric Supply and Aim Lighting in Plant City, Florida.

We profiled Steve in our first book. He's the energetic Alabama native who in 1996 brought to life a dream he'd had since grade school by opening his own electrical supply business.

His business was one we couldn't forget. Perhaps it was the upbeat attitude of the employees who answered the telephone each time we called. Maybe it was those 25-cent Cokes (the six-ounce kind that taste the best) and complimentary water, coffee and doughnuts that Steve kept on hand for customers. But most likely it was Steve himself, as down-to-earth a dreamer as you'd ever meet.

Steve dispels the notion that in order to live our dreams we must push aside reality, practicality and circumspection, and dive in spontaneously, eyes squeezed tightly shut against naysayers and doubters.

Although there is an undercurrent of danger in any business venture, Steve has reduced his risk through thoughtful research, persistent planning and constant inquiry of others. He's shown that in order to dream effectively, we need more than passion. We must also exercise patience, persistence and the ability to alter plans in the face of new information.

We last talked with Steve in the summer of 1998. His company had just turned two, still an infant in business terms. He was doing well, with four times the customers he'd projected to have 24 months into his business.

Yet, as statistics often remind us, few new small businesses survive, many closing within their first year. Aim Electric had made it past that point, but how would the company be doing in year three? We decided to check in with Steve. We were anxious to see if his progressive, customer friendly approach and innovative ideas were still making his business thrive. And, of course, we wanted to see what Steve had learned through the many years it had taken him to reach his dream.

The news was good, better perhaps than even Steve would have predicted. Earlier in 1999, Aim Electric had moved into larger quarters—a 1940s structure that once housed the first Oldsmobile dealership in Plant City. Situated prominently on Highway 92, Aim's new home is four times larger than the building it had been renting, which was hidden in an industrial area off the main byway.

That's not all that's new. In the all-glass showroom, where Florida sunshine once sparkled on the shiny metallic fins of classy Olds sedans, dazzling lighting fixtures dangle from the ceiling. This is the home of Steve's latest venture, Aim Lighting, run by his wife, Debbie. It was a move that just seemed natural, given the company's wholesale business and its new wealth of space.

"It was our accountant David's idea that instead of putting our existing service counter in the showroom, we use it for a lighting showroom," Steve said. "I had thought about one day opening up a lighting showroom, but I must admit David was the first to vocalize it and say, 'Gee, why don't we go ahead and do it!'

"There's been a lot of consolidating in the wholesale electrical supply business over the last decade or so, and as they got bigger and bigger the lighting showrooms didn't fit in, so they closed them down," Steve says. "So, we have very few competitors."

The retail operation has also given him the opportunity to advertise to a broader audience and to let the community know not only about his lighting business, but also about Aim Electric.

Steve has exhibited his typical conservative manner with the opening, keeping the cost of the new venture low by using existing employees and negotiating agreeable terms with suppliers. It's typical of his start-ups, growing slowly and surely as business warrants.

Although we've pegged Steve as a prudent businessman, he, like all entrepreneurs, is not without a smidgen of impulsiveness. He's learned that gut feelings are often worth his attention.

Steve had been eyeing Aim's new home for three years, driving past it almost daily, thinking it would be a perfect expansion vehicle for his business someday. Debbie was doing and thinking the same thing. Drive-by dreaming. You've gotta love it!

Then, one day late in 1998, Steve didn't just drive by the building. Instead, he pulled into the parking lot.

"There was a welding company in the building and the building was not for sale," Steve remembers. "After driving by it for three years, I just pulled in the parking lot one day, walked in the front door, introduced myself and said, 'If you are interested in selling, I'm interested in buying.'

"They said, 'Today is your lucky day. We'd love to move to Polk County (the next county over).'"

We love hearing about those kinds of "magical" moments. Over the years, we've discovered that what appears at first to be pure luck seems to involve much more than that. Call it synergy. Call it intuition. Call it just plain good timing. But we've noticed that if you stay true to your dream, and just keep plugging away, doors *do* open—sometimes as if by magic.

But if you think this latest dream fulfilled marks the end of Steve's dreams, well, just remember what we said earlier about chain reactions.

"I want to own a number of businesses," Steve says. "For one, it's more exciting and interesting. And, from an economic standpoint, I went through 1975, 1982 and 1991—and I don't know when the next recession is coming, but I've been through three and I don't want a single-faceted business that is reliant on a recession-crippled customer base."

His next business will be one that can profit from consumers whose purchasing power has been paralyzed by a recession's woes. It will be called Aim Rental and will rent equipment, tools and other items. "Obviously in a recession, people are more willing to rent than to buy," Steve says.

Like most business people, Steve's business acumen is a compilation of past experiences. In his case there have been three major influences—an ever-changing childhood home, a sixth-grade civics lesson and an entrepreneur named Clyde Reaves.

Because his father worked in construction, Steve's family was always on the move, following good weather and the building activity that accompanied it.

"When I graduated, it was from the twelfth school I had attended," Steve says. "There were times when we moved because Dad got transferred, times we moved because he got fired. So, there were times when we would have decent places to live and there were times when I definitely lived on the wrong side of the tracks."

Steve was the rare kid in the mid-1970s who had short hair by his father's decree. It made him stand out in each new school he attended, and, as he says, "It caused more than one problem."

Although it wasn't an easy way to live, it made Steve adaptive. Although it's a life he has purposely avoided subjecting his two children to, he's found that his roving childhood actually has given him some advantages.

"I learned how to meet people and go into a new environment and feel comfortable," he says. "I'm sure it gave me some people skills I wouldn't have had otherwise, and it made me feel comfortable in situations where maybe I'm the only one coming from a different perspective, because I was like that an awful lot growing up."

While Steve doesn't remember the teacher's name or face, he does remember the sixth-grade civics lesson that spawned his dream of owning his own business. "I learned about unions and the fact that everybody got a raise when everybody else got a raise, and you got to move up when someone retired and left an opening and not when you deserved it," he says.

He decided owning his own business was the best way to avoid that sort of work life. His kick start came in his teenage years, when he met a man who was living the dream he one day hoped to live himself.

Clyde Reaves was Debbie's next-door neighbor. She also baby-sat for the Reaves family, and Steve, her boyfriend at the time, spent a lot of time around the Reaves home. Over the years, Steve watched as Reaves started up business after business—self-serve car washes, windshield repair services, rental property, trailer parks. He asked questions and took mental notes. Much of what he learned through Reaves is evident in his business philosophy today.

"Here was a man who was in business on his own, starting things from the ground up and making things happen," Steve says. "He taught me about the possibility of owning numerous businesses so that if one suffered a setback, you would have income from the others. He also showed me that he could start from nothing and create a business. I always thought if Clyde could do it, I can do it."

A CONVERSATION WITH STEVE LAMBERT . . .

Embarking on a dream can be a scary proposition. Do you think fear is the biggest enemy when it comes to realizing your dreams?

I don't think fear is the biggest enemy. I think the big enemy is a steady paycheck. When you have a steady paycheck, you don't have near the impetus to take that leap. If you didn't have a steady paycheck, you'd be a lot less fearful of taking that leap. I think a steady paycheck keeps more people from starting their own business than anything else. The boom in small business starts that we've seen can be directly attributed to layoffs by the major U.S. corporations.

When you decided to expand your business, you took a big financial leap.

Yes, but I have a supportive banker and he knew when I told him the price that it was a very good deal. It's a small community bank, which is what I recommend to every small business person I talk to, because you get to develop a relationship with the banker and the banker has a sense of what's going on in the community. I also have a relationship with a large bank. They have people they call relationship bankers, who are supposed to be my contact. Well, in 12 years I've had eight relationship bankers. I don't want to place my business in a position where they're going to have a change in personnel, and all of a sudden that new person frowns on my business.

Is the willingness to take the leap perhaps the key component in realizing any dream?

No. You have to have the willingness to take the leap, but I don't think that's the big deal. I think the big deal is sticking through the problems once you've made the leap. I see so many make the leap, but then the first or second time they run into problems, they stop. There are going to be problems, and it's not something people think about.

When people decide to open their own business like me, most of the advice they are going to get will be negative, because the majority of businesses close down in the first year. They run into problems and they say, "Oh, this is what they were talking about. OK, so it is kind of expected that I shut down. So I'll shut down." These problems just confirm all the bad stuff they've heard.

So what can they do to avoid falling into that trap?

One, they can avoid the problem by recognizing it. What I've tried to do is to know there are going to be problems and try to anticipate as many as I can and try to work so that if I have a problem, it will be a relatively small one.

How does that work?

If I make the decision to only sell to people who pay their bills a month after I sell something to them, I am keeping myself from the big problem of selling a big order to somebody who pays in 90 days and plays havoc with my cash flow. Another example is that I try so hard to hire the right people, knowing that if I make a mistake it will be a lot more costly to fix the mistake of making a bad hire than it would be to wait until the right person comes along. It's trying to manage the situation so you have little problems and not big ones.

By watching Clyde Reaves, your friend the entrepreneur, did you pick up anything beyond the nuts and bolts of doing business?

Absolutely. You have to look at his attitude, his persistence, his patience. He would sit back and wait for the right opportunities to come along. You have to have the patience to do that. They typically happen because someone else has messed up. If you wait and watch for it, an opportunity will come along and it will be a no-brainer.

It seems your experience with Clyde shows why having a role model is important for someone who has a dream.

Certainly to witness someone doing what you've thought about doing clarifies some things in your mind as to what they did, how they did it, how you would do it, how you might do it differently. It just puts you in a much better position to do it successfully.

One of the things I have done over the years is invite another business owner to lunch to just discuss business and compare notes. Typically, the way I begin the conversation is, I ask them about their career and how they got where they are. I've learned so much just by asking that question. It is so open-ended it leads to all kinds of places.

Have their stories and case histories had an effect on your business?

I can tell you some general themes, such as, no matter how tempting it is, make sure you aren't selling to people who aren't going to pay you on time. You always have opportunities to sell to people who aren't going to pay you on time, and it is a daily chore to say no. You identify them from experience and by asking them questions, from belonging to the local credit association, by being observant and using your good common sense.

Another theme I hear over and over in talking with business folks is, keep your gross margins up and resist the temptation for the big sale and the low gross margin rate. Sales don't pay the bills. It's that gross margin dollar that does. Your costs can quickly jump up to match or exceed the gross margin dollars that come in. "Cheap business," I call it. It's kind of like those old boys that went down to the farm and bought watermelons for a dollar and went into town and sold them for a dollar, and couldn't understand why they weren't making any money. So they decided they needed to buy a bigger truck.

You took every opportunity to make yourself a better manager—working on an MBA, taking advantage of every training program the company you worked for offered. What did you learn about managing people?

If you are trying to select a person, you see if they have had that thread of success in the past. If they do, they are probably going to continue that. If they historically have shown poor judgment, they are probably going to have poor judgment. By the time I see them as adults, I as a manager can't change them. If we are trying to fill a particular job, then you try to figure out what type of person would best be rewarded by this job, and then you go try to find a person with those types of behavior. If I have something that is very detail-oriented, I need to find somebody who really feels good today if they have been able to get into those details. You ask questions, you find out what they like to do, what they are good at, what they've been good at in the past, and you look for trends.

You had your dream in the sixth grade. You were 39 before you made it come true. Why did you wait so long?

First of all, I was learning about business and I was improving my skills where I was. Second, the business I'm in requires a significant amount of capital and I saved for many years. I wanted to fund most of the business myself. I was always under the assumption that it would be difficult or impossible to get a bank to give me money or a loan as a start-up business. They would say, "Here's a person who hasn't run a business for himself before and he wants to do what?" So, when I did it, I wanted to be able to do most of it myself.

Did waiting so long ever frustrate you?

I am very comfortable with the time frame. I was taking advantage of every opportunity I had to learn when I was working for other people. I started investing in the stock market in the early 1980s when it was in the 1200s, and every piece of money I could, I put in a mutual fund.

Saving so diligently required some sacrifices, we suppose.

You give up the immediate. You give up the toys. I never have drooled over them, thank goodness. This dream of the business has always been much stronger for me than to have a nice boat or a recreational vehicle or take expensive vacations, or all these other numerous things that we could have spent the money on right away.

I look at my personal financial condition, and far and away the most important thing from one year to the next has been how much my net worth increased because I was trying to build a value that I could do something with.

Were there any temptations along the way? Was it ever difficult to stick with your program?

Yes, yes. During the recessions of 1982 and 1991 it was very difficult. But recessions only last for a short period of time, and I know that. I fully expect another recession. I don't know when it is going to be, but I certainly am managing Aim in a way that when it comes, we are going to be one of the survivors.

How do you build a business for a recession that has not arrived?

You build a customer base and a supplier base that you feel are the type of businesses that will be there and last through a recession. Let's look at what I haven't done. I haven't built Aim as a business based on commercial or residential construction. It would be tempting because there is huge money in that right now. The efforts we would expend to really grow that part of our business we could expend building a base of customers that will be there.

For example, when we go through the next recession, the hospital is still going to be treating folks; they'll still need supplies. Locally, there are distribution centers for grocery store chains. People are still going to be buying food. You just follow that train of thought. There are all kinds of commercial businesses out there that will just continue right along for the most part through a recession, and that's the type of customers you want—or at least that I want.

I am not going to stray from the path and go for the quick bucks. That's one of the reasons I tried to put aside a nest egg, because I know you don't go out and open the door and become immediately successful. I can remember times after we first opened, I'd pick up the telephone to make sure there was still a dial tone.

Was it really that slow at first?

Oh, sure. I opened on March 1. I didn't make my first sale until March 11. My total sales for the first month were $600.

Isn't that enough to devastate some people?

I guess, if they expected to go out and do wonderful things. The comfort was in knowing that I've done this work for 20 some odd years, and I thought I was pretty good at it. I was investing in myself, and I didn't know of any investment I felt more comfortable with. I knew how to do it, and I was going to try to do the right thing. If you can't bet on yourself, who can you bet on?

After that first month, how did you feel?

Great! I was on my own. The biggest thing was getting started. I had done it. And I felt great. I can imagine there may be people who would go into it without a business plan and think that what they dreamed is going to happen, but I wasn't like that.

I think it's a process of taking a dream and turning a dream into a reality. You have to think through and work through what you need to do to get it as close to realistic as you can justify on a piece of paper. I think people who start a business should write down what it is they want to do, and go talk to some business people and say, "This is what I want to do, what do you think about that?" They'll get more input than they can possibly imagine into the good, the bad and the ugly. But I think a lot of people don't want to go and ask for that advice.

Why?

Because they are scared of what they will hear. "Don't mess with my dream. I have my dream and it is so and so and that is the way it's going to be."

Yes, but can't negative input sometimes destroy someone's dream?

Yeah, but would you rather be shot down before you go through the monetary, physical and emotional investment, or would you rather do it and then be shot down? I think people who want to go into business for themselves should always look into it by considering that one of the options is, "Don't do it." I think a lot of people look into it and they don't consider that an option. And sometimes the option is "Don't do it now, go back, rethink it, come back, ask more questions, do it later."

Did anyone tell you that you shouldn't do this?

Oh, absolutely. I had people telling me I was stupid because I opened in a town with a population of approximately 30,000, and in the 1970s and 1980s there had been two other electrical distributors who had opened and closed here. I think the biggest difference between us and them is that they opened here to do business here, and to succeed or fail here. We opened to do business here and the rest of west central Florida. We never limited ourselves to just this 30,000 population base.

How did it make you feel when people shot down your idea?

The first thing you do is get mad. And the second thing you think is, "Why are they saying that, and could they be right?" The third thing you think is, "Hey, I thought this through. I did the market research and even though Plant City might not support what I want to do with Aim, it will be a wonderful starting point. Sitting right here by the interstate, as Tampa and Orlando grow closer together, it will be an excellent location to serve this big market." And I just have to figure that those people aren't thinking that far ahead.

Why did you realize it was important to hear things like that?

Anytime you ask people's opinions, you should expect to hear positive and negative. And when they tell you the negative, after you've finished getting upset, then you need to think about it. Why did they say that? What truth is there to it? Are they saying that based on their own experiences? Sometimes they are right, or there's a piece of something they are saying that is right.

People who don't want to share their dream might be unwilling to do so because they don't want to change their dream.

I think that while you may be reluctant to adjust the end result of the dream, you must be willing to adjust your plans to get there.

Do you ever see small business people who fail because they are not this flexible?

Yes. I think they make the mistake of thinking if they compromise on how they go about achieving their dream, then they've compromised their dream. And I think it is two different things.

Your work day is hectic. When do you find time to dream new dreams?

It's difficult to do it during the day. So you have to make time for it. It's like I need a fix of it. If I go too many days without reflecting on where we are versus where we want to be, I have to get some time. At least 30 minutes. That's how I gauge whether or not we are where we need to be. I pull back out pieces of paper with plans and goals written on them and refresh my memory.

A lot of new business owners find it difficult to find the time to do this.

Yes. They are fighting the alligators and they don't take the time to reflect, to make sure what they are doing is what they originally intended to do. And if they're not, they need to ask if they've changed course for good reasons.

What does it take to live the dream of being a business owner?

You have to be comfortable with a certain amount of risk. You have to be comfortable occasionally going to sleep not knowing how you are going to cover that check you wrote today. I think some people like the sense of being comfortable more so than the risk involved. There are plenty of us who feel this great sense of accomplishment, but I also think there are a lot of people who don't need that. They feel better just being comfortable. I think those of us who want to start our own business like a little discomfort.

There is one thing, though. When you are out on your own it is much, much more difficult to develop that circle of people where you pick up the phone or walk down the hall and ask their opinion of something. I've been able to get that through membership in the Chamber of Commerce, contact with the Small Business Development Center and my involvement in the Rotary Club and my church.

Who else has had influence on your life?

Definitely my wife, Debbie. She is the one who has smoothed the rough edges. Growing up, going to all those schools, I had to be fairly outspoken and aggressive to survive, and not all of that was good. You need to know when to keep your mouth shut and when to say things in a nicer way. She, more than anyone else, has helped me do that. She certainly reminded me when I had made a boo-boo. I very much appreciate it. I needed that.

And my high school football and wrestling coach, Tom Grant in Jacksonville, Florida. He tried to instill in me the desire to win. Although I was a pretty good performer for him, what he was trying to teach me didn't click until I was in my mid-20s. I had been working and being successful, but I wouldn't say I was putting forth any more than a normal effort. Then, for some reason, that competitive desire clicked in, and from then on it has been an all-out push for what can I learn, get better at and do something with. I really owe him a lot.

How do you get others to buy into your dream?

I'm constantly telling employees, customers and suppliers what those dreams are—not only telling them what they are, but how I intend to do something about them and why I think they will unfold. I think that really helps people buy in.

Does it help you?

Oh yes, absolutely. If you say something that's really dumb, they catch you on it. And you have to rethink it.

How about inspiration?

It's always there. I'm constantly being fed by large and small successes. I don't have to go looking for it because it is always being fed. When we've worked hard or an employee has reached another milestone or some customer has complimented us—there's just these little successes all the time. I don't need any more inspiration than that.

Those compliments from customers mean a lot more than a plaque on the wall.

Absolutely. If you saw my office, you'd see there are zero plaques. I've got some, but they are at home in the attic. I don't want any of them up. I guess what I thrive on is seeing, hearing and being part of these small successes, and it really doesn't matter much if someone else thinks that I did something good.

If you were going to advise someone on the secret to developing a dream, what would you tell them?

Number one is, write it down. Number two is discuss with others who have done it, and listen to what they say. Three, read and study all you can about it. Number four is, take all that information and focus it down. Each part of the dream has to stand on its own.

The final thing is a word I use constantly: anticipate. How do you get better at it? You practice it.

Tom Roberts (center) and his many faces (clockwise from top): as Teddy Roosevelt, Santa Claus, Gutzon Borglum, and Scrooge.

5

TOM ROBERTS
ACTOR, TEACHER, VOLUNTEER

"If we can dream, we have hope.
If we have hope, life has possibilities."

Tom Roberts knew at an early age that he had a special love for performing. He especially loved the great comic actors. Huge talents like Peter Sellers, Jonathan Winters, Dick Van Dyke, Cary Grant and Red Skelton made lasting impressions by giving him a deep appreciation for what humor and laughter can do to lift the human spirit.

But Tom also knew that he wanted to be a teacher. There's always been a flame inside him, a desire to teach and to share. His challenge, then, was to find a way to merge these two seemingly divergent roads into a single path. The problem was, he had no role models to follow. There weren't (and still aren't) a lot of actors in South Dakota, and neither his parents, both of whom were hardworking farmers, nor his siblings had anything beyond a passing interest in the arts.

Tom Roberts had a flame inside him, but no one to help him light the torch.

Then Mark Twain came along and changed all that—or, more accurately, Hal Holbrook in his one-man show as the great American writer and humorist.

"Yeah, I was in college when I saw a clip of Hal Holbrook doing Mark Twain," Tom says. "I was immediately hooked. And what hooked me was that it had all aspects of performing. Acting, writing, makeup . . . it was all present in that single one-man show. Plus, Hal Holbrook was teaching us through the words of Mark Twain. I knew right then that I had discovered a way to do exactly what I wanted to do, and that I could do it by being a performing artist."

The result has been a long and gratifying career that's allowed Tom not only to realize his dream, but also help others find theirs—sometimes in ways he hardly could have imagined. The stage on which Tom performs is often anything but traditional. He works in prisons, nursing homes, elementary schools . . . almost anywhere, really. Besides performing, he provides workshops and encouragement to others. The result is that his audiences don't just sit and watch. They often become involved. And in some cases—like the nursing homes, or the prisons—they come alive again.

Tom went to college at Northern State University in Aberdeen, South Dakota, majoring in speech and theater. It was there, surrounded by a group of energetic and like-minded friends, that his talents began to bloom.

"My love for the arts began when I was really quite young," Tom remembers. "I'm not sure why I was so drawn to the arts, but I was. I did a few plays in high school, but it wasn't until I got to college that I really began to get involved in a deeper, more serious way. I look back on those times as being very enjoyable."

Tom began his career while still in college. One of his first shows? You guessed it, performing as Mark Twain. Another early effort was a one-man show as Will Rogers. It's no accident that Tom used the words of those two American icons to lay the foundation for his career. The reason, he says, is the humor.

"I'm firmly convinced that the importance of humor in our lives can't be overemphasized," Tom says. "That's true in all aspects of life, and it's especially true when trying to teach. If you can instill some humor into whatever it is you're trying to do, you have a much better chance of succeeding. And believe me, I've been in some places where humor is in short supply and desperately needed—and, I might add, greatly appreciated by those who are on the receiving end."

As Tom's reputation grew, and as more and more job offers came his way, he expanded his cast of characters, adding, among others, Theodore Roosevelt, Ebenezer Scrooge and Badger Clark, the South Dakota poet. During a celebration at Mt. Rushmore, Tom did a highly successful one-man show as Gutzon Borglum, the man responsible for that marvelous American monument.

Despite his continuing success as an actor, never was Tom tempted by the bright lights of Broadway or the glitter of Hollywood. While virtually every actor dreams of making it big in either or both of those performing meccas, Tom says he never gave it serious thought. For him, Sioux Falls was the perfect home base.

"Never even considered it," Tom says of relocating. "I know that may sound strange, but it just wasn't the way I wanted to go. I've known too many people who have taken that route and ended up terribly unhappy and unfulfilled. I was perfectly content to stay in South Dakota and do my work here. And I was very fortunate to make a good enough name for myself so that I kept getting work.

"Let's face it, what I do is rather unique. There just aren't many people who do it. And that's especially true in South Dakota. The state isn't being overrun by performing artists. Because of that, I've been able to carve out my own niche here. As long as I could make a living in South Dakota, there really wasn't any need for me to leave."

There was another crucial factor in Tom's decision to remain in his home state—his wife Tammy works as the Director of Marketing at a local college.

Tom also thumbed his nose at another time-honored actor's tradition by refusing to hire an agent. He chose instead to work as a true freelance performer, relying on his reputation—and the uniqueness of what he does—to generate enough word of mouth buzz to keep the phone ringing.

One reason why Tom is able to stay busy is his great versatility. He isn't simply a one-man show, he's a one-man theater company. He can literally do it all. Along with acting, he's a skilled and creative makeup artist. He's constantly in demand to do voice-overs for TV and radio, and to work in industrial videos. And in recent years, as if acting and makeup weren't enough, he's added writing and directing to his list of credits.

Tom hasn't always worked alone. Far from it, in fact. Several years ago, he and Bob Wyant formed Harvest Moon Productions with the express purpose of touring the state doing a series of two-man shows. It's been a successful and satisfying partnership. Wyant, who wrote the lyrics for The Guess Who's song "These Eyes," and Tom are currently touring in a two-man comedy titled *Greater Tuna*.

Another of Tom's partners is Pam Donelan, whom Tom describes as "a feisty Irish nun with a great sense of humor." She helps Tom create programs for health care conferences. Their company is called Sightlines Productions.

For Tom, though, the greatest satisfaction comes from teaching. There is nothing he enjoys more, or gives him a greater sense of fulfillment, than to use the arts as a way to teach. That's why he cringes anytime he hears that funds for the arts have been cut.

"Historically, the arts are always the first to be cut back," Tom says. "That's a sad reality that we have to live with. And yet, when studies are done, one consistent conclusion is that the arts are very important to learning. Naturally, I tend to agree with that conclusion.

"One of the greatest obstacles I've had to face is getting people to accept the arts as something more than entertainment. Oftentimes I felt like my sponsors wanted me to be nothing more than a glorified baby sitter. But the arts can be a learning tool, a healing tool, and it can also be a lot of fun. That's something I've always tried to do—to make whatever I do a fun experience as well as a learning experience."

Tom has several different venues in which he uses his performing arts' skills as learning tools—schools, correctional facilities and, more recently, health care facilities.

For the past 16 years, the majority of Tom's time has been spent in artist-in-school residencies. The Arts in the Schools

Program was developed by the South Dakota Arts Council, and has been highly successful. Tom goes into a school, works with students from kindergarten through grade 12, and, in many instances, does in-service training with the teachers.

"The way it usually goes is that I'm hired to go into a school, usually for a week or two," Tom says. "My focus is to develop a better understanding and appreciation of what the performing arts are."

Tom says dealing with students ranging from K through 12 presents some unique challenges.

"The younger kids, K through second or third grade, have very short attention spans, which means you can't work with them for long periods of time," he says. "The older students are by far the most challenging. I have to get them to trust me before they'll invest their time and energy in what we're trying to do. The ideal age group is third through sixth or seventh grade. I love working with them. They're attentive, receptive to ideas, just a great age group to work with."

With teachers, Tom says, the goal is to help them develop a fresh perspective and lose their fear of using fun and games as productive ways of teaching.

"I try to demonstrate to teachers, counselors, therapists and managers that the lessons I'm teaching go beyond the stage," he says. "Communication skills, character development skills, physical control and interrelationship skills can be taught in an innovative manner that is inviting and fun to learn."

Another program that Tom helped developed is the Youths at Risk Program. Over the years he has performed in numerous prisons and correctional facilities. Once, while preparing for a show, he spent time studying the guards and inmates in San Quentin.

And would you believe that inmates prove to be one of the best groups to work with?

"I can almost always count on getting a good reception at a prison or correctional facility," Tom says. "I've found them to be the ideal students. To begin with, they know this is something special when it comes in. They are very attentive, and they ask great questions. When I work in those places, I use a lot of humor and I keep it fast paced. My main objective is to build self-esteem. We work on things like body language and how to build teamwork and relationships."

The latest venue to capture Tom's attention, and one that he is passionate about, is health care facilities. Working with the sick and disabled is something Tom says he wants to explore even more in the future. It's his firm belief that the performing arts can be a healing mechanism.

Tom says some of his most memorable moments have come while working with the elderly and the disabled.

"Once, while working with a group of older developmentally disabled men and women, I thought it would be fun to demonstrate some makeup," Tom remembers. "The majority of this group were non-verbal, very low comprehension, and had difficulty hearing. As I spoke, a tall gentleman rose and walked up to me, pulled up a chair directly in front of me and sat down facing away. I've learned to expect bizarre behavior in such situations, so I wasn't bothered by his actions. Instead, I began applying makeup to him. When I concluded, I took a hand mirror and showed him what he looked like. I'd made him up to look like Groucho Marx. He looked in the mirror, then up at me. Then he put his hand to his mouth as if he were twiddling a cigar, smiled and rolled his eyes, *a la* Groucho. The audience cheered. He spent the next half hour going up and down the halls, peeking into each room and showing off his new face.

"On another occasion, an elderly lady with a frail voice read a wonderful poem she wrote about her mother. When she finished, the room exploded with applause. One of the staff members asked her if she knew any more poems, and the lady said, 'Lots.' When someone asked her why she had never shared these things before, the lady replied, 'Nobody asked me before.'

"In moments like those, I'm witness to self-discoveries that resonate far beyond those individuals. The other patients, the staff, even the families of these individuals who hear about it later are all enriched by these shared creative gifts. For me, it was a reminder to not be presumptuous, and that everyone has something creative to contribute. Sometimes all we have to do is ask, to give them the tools to express themselves."

That's a lesson, we think, that leaders in business or in any kind of organization can put to use as well.

Clearly, Tom Roberts is one of the lucky ones. He's had the perseverance and good fortune to live life on his terms and to see his lifelong dream come true. He's made a living doing what he loves, and he's shared his talent and skills with others. More important, he's made a difference.

And he's not through yet. He has new and fresh ideas for the future, one of which is to work with Tammy, who also happens to be an accomplished performer and an excellent singer.

Tom's great contributions have not gone unrewarded. Over the years, he's received numerous national and state honors, including the Sioux Falls Outstanding Arts Award (three times) and South Dakota's Emerging Artist Award. In 1991, Tom was recognized by Gov. George Mickelson and the U.S. Post Office for his work during the Golden Anniversary celebration at Mt. Rushmore. And in 1994, he was honored for his contributions as a theater instructor at the annual Donna Reed Festival, becoming one of a handful of non-celebrities to have his hand prints set in cement for permanent display.

But as Tom is quick to say, awards and honors are nice, but they're only icing on the cake.

"I love what I'm doing, and I can see myself doing it for a long time," he says. "I've had to worry at times because I never knew what the income would be from year to year. But I've stuck it out. People know me and trust me. I've always given people a sense of consistency, and that's why they kept calling me.

"I've always viewed life as one long learning experience. A continuing challenge and adventure. It never gets boring. It gets difficult at times, but never boring."

A CONVERSATION WITH TOM ROBERTS . . .

What's the idea or quality that sets you apart?

My perspective on taking things as they come. To not let challenges get me down. That's something I've had to work very hard at. To not beat myself up when things go bad, which they often do.

Who is the person—or mentor—who has influenced you the most in your work and in your life?

I'm not sure it's any one person. My father and uncle, with their great passion for the outdoors, certainly influenced me in that area. My mother and grandmother influenced me with their great sense of humor and their sense of compassion to help others. And my brother Jim has been a big influence. He's always been there for me. I credit him with helping me with my character.

Can you think of a time when you were able to take a rigid program and tailor it in such a way that it worked to your advantage?

When I was contracted to go to the Federal Prison Camp, I had to create and fashion a program. I had to develop the entire thing by myself. I spent nine months there, studying the routine of the guards, the prisoners, everybody. And you know what I discovered? The inmates had a strong interest in poetry. We had a series of poetry readings. It turned out to be a terrific experience.

Where did the idea to work in correctional facilities come from?

During my years of conducting Artist in School residencies, I had occasionally been asked to work with at-risk youth at social service agencies and juvenile detention centers. When the South Dakota Arts Council received a grant to create a residency program (ArtsCorr) in the state juvenile correctional facilities, I was asked to be a participating artist.

When the Yankton Federal Prison Camp received a grant from the National Endowment for the Arts to conduct a pilot artist-in-residence program, I was again asked to be involved. I had the experience and the willingness to use my art medium as a means of teaching positive communications skills and self-awareness.

Working in a prison is a lot different than working in an elementary school. Did you receive any special training before you went in?

Yes. I was sent for training at San Quentin Prison and the Duel County Correctional Facility in California, where they have had great success in creating various arts programs that have had a constructive impact on the inmates. When I returned, I had the opportunity to spend nearly a year at the Yankton Federal Prison Camp, where I experimented with various programs involving classes, performances and reader's theater.

Was that effort a success?

Very much so, yes. When I finished my residency there, the inmates put together a handmade going-away gift for me. It was a plaque, to which was attached a rock with a monarch butterfly perched on top of it, appearing as if it were ready to take flight. On the wooden base, there was a four-leaf clover that one of the inmates found on the grounds. Along with it, they gave me a card that read, "Thank you for setting our spirits free!"

How were you initially received by the prison or camp leaders?

Some of the administrators and teachers confessed to me that they were reluctant to bring in a theater artist because they were expecting someone who was more effeminate, and that they were surprised that I wasn't.

When I was asked to conduct a residency at the Custer Boot Camp (a state-run juvenile correctional facility), the Colonel wanted to meet with me because he was concerned about the activities that I might have in store for the cadets. He even sat in on several of my early sessions, just observing. He must have liked what I did because this past year he had me conduct a similar session with 30 of his Boot Camp drill instructors.

Prisons and correctional facilities aren't normally associated with dreams. How do you get the inmates to begin to dream again?

I once read somewhere that "Liberty defines our physical boundaries, but freedom is a state of mind where there are no boundaries." It is my belief that if we can dream, we have hope. If we have hope, life has possibilities. If life has possibilities, then we should prepare ourselves for the moment when opportunity knocks. Meanwhile, let's encourage each other to dream.

When I was at San Quentin, I worked with a group of male inmates, many of whom were serving life sentences. As they entered, I thought they were a team of World Wrestling Federation contestants. But I suspected that there was a child's heart in each one of them.

We talked informally for a while, then I informed them that it was important to tap into the creative energy of the child that dwells within each of us. I had them rise and stand in a circle. For the next three hours, we did creative drama, improvisations, characterizations and dramatic readings, all of which they participated in with great delight. We laughed, joked and just enjoyed the spirit of the moment.

What about working in health care facilities? What triggered that?

My high school drama teacher, who happens to be a Catholic Presentation Sister, called me up one day and asked if I would help her out as a co-presenter at a conference for a local hospital. I accepted. Thus began a very enjoyable working relationship that has lasted for almost seven years. Together, we create customized programs for various health care facilities based on their history, their accomplishments, their challenges and their aspirations. Our programs generally target administrators, managers and employees, but we eventually hope to produce programs for patients as well.

What are the Sioux Falls and South Dakota arts communities like?

Being a predominantly rural state, South Dakota doesn't have the resources or the facilities to attract a lot of artists, arts organizations or large arts events. However, the arts here continue to grow in quantity, quality and general acceptance. Community Arts Councils around the state have increased considerably in numbers and activities over the past decade. In particular, I have seen the Sioux Empire Arts of Sioux Falls blossom and become a vibrant resource for this community.

You use humor to great effect in your programs. Can you recall any specific instances where you've had humorous interactions with students or prisoners?

One time when I was doing makeup demonstrations for a group of young people, a little 5-year-old girl marched up to me and asked if I would make her look like a clown. I said OK, and before I could say another word she plops down on the stool in front of me and begins to tell me exactly how I should commence. She said, "I'll need a red nose! Clowns always have a red nose! And red lips that look like a big smile! Can you do that?" When I nodded my head, she continued on with her specific directions, saying, "Then I think my eyes should be blue with green eyebrows. And then I'll need a big fuzzy wig." I told her I could do all of that. Then I asked her what color her cheeks should be. She hadn't considered that. She thought for a moment, then looked up at me and said, "I don't know. You decide. You're the expert!"

You said that you've had to struggle against beating yourself up at times. How have you learned to deal with those times when you have failed, when the dream is obscured by the current situation?

By always trying to surround myself with supportive people. And I also try to let go of whatever it is that's bothering me as soon as possible. But without question, the most important thing is that my family and friends have always been there for me.

How have you been able to overcome fear of action?

By trying as much as possible to be like my brother Jim. He's always willing to take on things. He's simply unafraid to try. If it doesn't work, you learn from it, then move on. I've tried to act the same way.

How important are the arts to children? How does it help them to dream?

The arts provide children of all ages an opportunity to stimulate, develop and strengthen their creative resources so that they can realize their full potential as an interactive participant in this earthly existence. The arts promote hope by teaching us to envision, imagine and explore, thereby fueling the fire of which dreams are made.

What are some other ideas you would like to implement?

I would like to continue to find new ways of applying my performing art skills in different environments. Perhaps hospitals, senior centers, corporations and community service agencies. I would like to write and produce more programs that lift people up and make them feel good about themselves as well as each other.

Can you think of an instance where you've had to overcome false perceptions?

I almost always have to do just that anytime I go to a school for the first time. When they hear that an actor—an artist—is coming, they look at me with a wary eye. They think I'll have long hair and talk with a lisp. It usually takes about two days before they change their opinion—or their preconceived notion—of me.

What are some ways you recharge your batteries?

I like my quiet time. Sometimes I like to drive or just go to the park. When I'm in the process of working on a new program, I'll just sit in the backyard with a pad and pencil and jot down thoughts.

Name your five favorite books of all time.

Oh, I would say the works of Hans Christian Andersen. A book called *Jacob the Baker* by Noah Ben Shea. *Winters' Tales* by Jonathan Winters. A book called *Chronicles of Courage*. And any Stephen Covey book.

How do you encourage others—maybe young people who want to become actors—to follow their dreams while still maintaining a certain focus on reality?

By telling them to keep a clear definition of what success really means. I tell them to not let theater become their life. To not try so hard. To enjoy it. That's when doors open. I'm a big fan of Stephen Covey. I love his idea of a mission statement. That's something I took to heart. I didn't want fame or money. Life is not fame and fortune. Life is here and now. I found something Emerson said that sums up my feelings. He said:

"A person is a success who has lived well, laughed often and loved much. Who has gained the respect of intelligent people and the love of little children. Who has found their niche and accomplished their task. Who has made the world a better place than they found it—whether it be by an improved flower, a perfect poem or a rescued soul. Who has never lacked appreciation of the earth's beauty or failed to express it. Who has always looked for the best in others and given the best they have. Whose life is an inspiration and whose memory is a benediction."

Pat and Jean Smith (top) during ceremony honoring Pat as Chief of Developmental Affairs. At bottom, the Smiths in their Lexington home, along with daughter Jennifer, son Brian and John Osei-Kwakye of Ghana.

6

PAT AND JEAN SMITH
FORMER BUSINESS
OWNERS, VOLUNTEERS

"If you have a passion for it,
you'll find a way to get it done."

I n a time when our lives are getting longer and the rate of change in our organizations and our lives is getting faster, it comes as no surprise that many people pursue multiple dreams. When one dream comes full circle, they use that experience to lay the groundwork for a new wave of growth.

We know a bit about what that's like at WYNCOM. In fact, our work could be described as a pattern of over-lapping dreams. The constant factors are the drive and desire of our nationally acclaimed speakers, our employees, our partners and our customers. In many cases, we have been fortunate to be a part of their personal journeys.

You might recall our profile of Patrick and Jean Smith in our previous book. Until recently, Pat was a principal owner and president of Software Information Systems, an Inc. 500 company that was recently accorded the honor of IBM Premier Business Partner. The company has been in operation since 1982 and underwent rapid expansion recently, with offices opening in two more cities in 1998.

In 1997 and twice more in 1998, the Smiths followed the example of Habitat for Humanity founders Millard and Linda Fuller by going on a Habitat mission to Africa, leading the effort to build several houses and taking on the immense project of a new community church for Assasan, Ghana.

Their spirit was contagious within their church and within their family. A son and daughter also made a mission trip, as well as dozens of others from their Lexington, Kentucky, community. Their parish raised over $50,000 for the various projects.

"It's affected my whole life," said Jean after their return from Africa in 1998. "I think about those people every day. I feel like whereas before our business was everything, this has just opened up my life. There's so much more that we can do."

So they're doing it.

Today, the Smiths stand on the precipice of another adventure. They've sold their interests in their surging company to colleagues through an internal buyout so they can pursue more fully their vocation with Habitat and the people of Ghana. At a stage in their careers when many are planning their exit strategies, they are entering a new world. And while they have accumulated a certain stake to back them up financially, they now have some "skin in the game" like never before.

We thought it would be good to catch up with Pat and Jean at this major turning point in their lives. Their first dream went from the two of them in their living room to 41 employees in five offices in three states. Now comes what is, in many respects, a bigger and bolder dream—one that the Smiths readily agree is fraught with unknowns, but one which has already enriched their lives in ways they could hardly have imagined.

Out in "the bush," the Smiths worked hand in hand with the villagers and other Habitat volunteers to build homes and the church (the old one had deteriorated so badly that all that remained was its bell tower). They saw women who would sit all day sifting pebbles for the making of cement. They'd join in by walking to the bore hole and filling head pans of water to use in mixing the cement for the blocks used to build the church.

They'd see each new block completed, and know that all of it had been done by hand—their hands, and the villagers' hands. Community.

The people of Assasan made Pat the village's Chief of Developmental Affairs. They had a big ceremony for the Smiths—Pat and Jean dressed in ceremonial garb, a pure gold bracelet around Pat's arm, held together by two old nails. No CEO title here—only a deep sense of belonging, of being part of something larger than themselves.

As the roof goes onto the new church in Assasan—a project completed in just over a year, when original forecasts according to normal Ghanaian construction standards called for nearly 20 years—Pat and Jean are looking at other projects, including the possibility of developing a U.S.-based distribution business to export goods made by homeowners in Ghana.

The idea isn't to turn the village into a mega export business—or alter the lifestyle and basic values of the village. After all, what drew the Smiths to more involvement with the village is in part its special character and sense of community. What they see, rather, is an opportunity to allow more people to build houses and make modest improvements in their lives.

Although Habitat for Humanity's mission has historically been tied exclusively to domestic shelter, Pat and Jean's idea is to set up income generating projects through another entity that would work in cooperation with Habitat affiliates.

"We've started a new company called Global HandWorks," Pat explains. "We want to fund projects of homeowners through their Habitat affiliates. They could set up a woodcarving business, for instance. Global HandWorks buys the carvings, exports them, then sells them in the U.S. If we can get Habitat to endorse it, the benefit would be that their homeowners get the bulk of the income, which improves their quality of life and allows them to make their house payments. That makes the local Habitat affiliate more successful, which should mean they'd be able to build more houses."

A non-export prototype of the project went into operation in 1998: a co-op bread oven, with the aim of generating income to open more co-ops. The hope is that working out the kinks in that setting will provide a model organization to replicate with other processes and products.

"If we could get Habitat to help promote the products, that would provide a potential market too," Smith continues. "You could replicate the co-op concept at affiliates all over the world. You could go to Eastern Kentucky, Asia, anywhere with this concept. The homeowner benefits, Habitat benefits, and they are promoted worldwide. It seems like a no-brainer, but we don't know yet."

As we met with the Smiths to talk again, another journey to Africa beckoned. The church was about to be dedicated, and the village planned to celebrate. "It's amazing how many people want to go back," says Jean. "Many people's children are going this time, too. Look at the hundreds of people involved in this project now: doctors, people at church, 600 kids at Christ the King school (in Lexington) who raised $6,000."

Like others with newly minted visions, the Smiths are sowing the seeds for dreamers beyond themselves. Not coincidentally, they've discovered that in deciding to help enrich the lives of others, their own lives are becoming fuller.

A CONVERSATION WITH PAT AND JEAN SMITH . . .

What sparked this new dream, this new direction?

PAT: I think over the six years I've worked with Habitat, I've always had the desire to really help others. It's been a one-shot deal each year for several weeks, and I've always enjoyed it. It comes from doing something for people without expectation of return. It's neat to feel like you've had involvement with helping people. It's something you can do and not look beyond it for satisfaction or reward.

We've been in a pretty stressful business: long hours, ever changing. I guess it just kind of got to me. The real decision to sell the business came from our first trip to Africa in 1997. Number one, it's humbling, and two, it makes you stop and think about what's important. Working hard and making money is not that important to us anymore. We need it to live comfortably, but it's not our prime motivation.

We came away from there having seen that sense of joy and happiness among those people who have nothing. It made us stop and think about what's important. I'm just amazed that literally hundreds of people have become involved with that church building. We raised $40,000 in less than 40 days. Twenty-three people have gone over there. We leave July 5 (1999) with another group of ten people, and plans call for Archbishop Turkson from Cape Coast, Ghana, to come for a dedication Mass.

How have your business associates and acquaintances reacted?

JEAN: Some were surprised that we were going. But they were behind us, and a lot of people gave us money for the Habitat houses and church. They didn't want to go, but if we were crazy enough to try it, they'd give the money to us.

PAT: From the work side, they understand that my interest has gone toward chasing another dream, and they've been very supportive of that. We've been looking for over a year at different ways to do it. We wanted to do it in a way that was most beneficial to everybody: owners, employees and customers. The best way was an internal buyout, which we did through an investor and some financing.

Some people are envious in a couple of ways: They're not convinced they could tolerate the environment there, or they don't have the means yet. I've talked to hundreds of people since we started this work, and I only got one comment from one person that was negative. He said, "With all those people over there without houses, what difference will one house make?" I said, "If you could see the faces of that one family when we dedicate that house, you'd know the difference one house makes."

You can write off a country of 20 million people if you want and say, "They've never had it and never will, so why help?" Or you can go after it one house at a time.

And some of those people don't realize the benefit such a project has to you personally.

PAT: Some people say, "Why spend all that money to go over there, why not just send the money over?" To that I say, "You're missing the point. The point is to help other people. That's the point of the whole thing."

JEAN: I think back to the hundreds of people who have gotten involved in this since we started, and that there might be a little change in the way they're thinking about doing things for others. Maybe they'll go volunteer in a nursing home for a couple of hours because of this project. That was Father Greg's (Greg Schuler, rector of Christ the King) thought when he supported the project.

Little things do have a ripple effect that we don't even realize at the time.

PAT: That's right. Our kids got real interested. They would never have gone if we had not done this. I'm real proud of them. Jennifer went, and she doesn't tolerate change of environment and food very well. My thinking was that it was not in her nature, but she went and loved every minute of it. In fact, she's going back with us in July. She has gotten engaged, and now she's going back with her fiancé, who I think saw what this experience has meant to her. Our son Brian would give anything to go back, too.

Father Charles Howell is going this time. He's 36, used to be a Baptist, and he was an assistant coroner here. He converted to Catholicism, then became a priest. He's a really interesting guy. A lot of people thought he shouldn't go last year, being a brand new priest, too risky. What if it all went down the tubes? Halfway through the trip, I was concerned he wouldn't want to come back, he was so at home there. He went because of always dreaming of doing mission work in Africa. He had a challenge last year there with a kidney stone, but he wants to go back. Father Charles is a guy with some dreams. I've seen him undergo quite a transformation in the year since he was ordained. He'll be a dynamite priest.

Another guy who went last year is going on another Habitat Global Village trip this summer to Russia. A lot of the people have done other things as a result of that initial experience.

Similarly, a lot of businesses are talking a lot more about investing their money and people in their own communities, doing group volunteer work, etc. What do you see as the best things to come out of this?

PAT: If a business owner understands the value of having employees involved in things like that, how it makes them better and happier people, in theory it would benefit everybody. Unfortunately, a lot of companies look at employees as bodies there to get things done, only there to generate revenue. They don't really care what they do outside of work.

Our employees were always our most valuable asset. The more well-rounded the employee, the better they will be. You'll have a better company that way. A lot of employers want to grow people professionally, but not so much personally.

A well-rounded view of life makes you a better person. A company needs to be good people first and foremost. As long as you promote those kinds of things, you'll have a successful company. You can get people to go build a house, for instance, and build camaraderie and teamwork. There are all kinds of intangibles that companies can derive that they often don't realize. Unfortunately, a lot of charitable contributions are made only for visibility.

"What am I going to get in return?" That's the wrong approach. The relationships and connections people make are what you get out of it.

What lessons have you carried back with you about our roles as citizens and neighbors?

PAT: I have a totally different appreciation of the people I respond to here now. And I have a different appreciation for the people in our government.

I think a lot of people treat our government officials like second-class, uncaring citizens, but you go over to Ghana or some other Third World country, and you see what they have and don't have and how things work. You pay bribes to go down roads. Police want bribes because they are not paid. Open sewers, electricity that may not work. Last July, we walked to a little village up the road for a cold beer after working hard all day. They only had warm ones, because the electricity went off a couple days earlier. Nobody knew why it went off or when it might come back on. Can you imagine what Lexington would do if that happened? Over there, they just didn't have it, and then they were happy to have it when they did have it.

Again, the neat thing about this whole project is not just to go someplace, but to get other people involved in this kind of work. If you step back and see the bigger picture, it's about getting people connected, whether it's a Saturday morning in Lexington, a weekend in Appalachia or going to Africa.

You both certainly made a lot of connections in building your company into such a success. Was founding SIS and watching it grow a dream realized?

PAT: The company far exceeded the wildest expectations we ever had. My first real job was working at the University of Kentucky, which like a lot of universities is a bureaucratic institution. I had a little more entrepreneurial spirit in me. When we talked about leaving, the first choice was to take a job in private industry. There were a lot of opportunities away from Lexington, but we didn't want to move. So we decided to go out on our own and try it.

Jean was the one who was probably more insistent on trying something on our own. She really wanted to stay here. We said we'd give it a try, give it a go. If it worked, fine, and if it didn't, we'd just have to reassess later. That's a lot of what you have to do.

My dream was to have a comfortable living with a small company. It grew to 41 employees, offices in five cities, and a dominant force within the market for IBM. And it has the potential to be far greater than that. It requires a lot of dedication and effort if you really want to grow it, and that just wasn't my focus anymore. But every year, it far exceeded expectations.

We started it in our living room here, with about $1,000 in our savings account. One client, one old Oldsmobile . . . that was the beginnings of our company. I don't think anybody can tell you they have this great dream and can see it being 50 employees. It evolved to that. But as it evolves, you do dream about it being a little bigger, a little more prominent.

Who have been some of your mentors, people who have helped show you the way?

PAT: On the business side, there were a number of people in IBM. I was intimidated early on, because I was a one-man operation, David and Goliath. I was one guy with an idea trying to do work for small clients, working with a massive organization called IBM. Learning what to do and also what not to do is important. They showed me both. They were a big, slow moving organization at one time, and especially in the technology industry today, you cannot be slow moving, bureaucratic and resistant to change, or you'll go by the wayside very quickly.

There were lots of clients who taught me: Jim Fisher with IBM, a good friend. He taught me how to always be positive, think positive. Host Communications had an impact on us, including Jim Host himself.

On the personal side, it hasn't been specific individuals, but more a sense of realizing the importance of doing those things like with Habitat, involvement with our church, and not forgetting the importance of helping others. People's lives are so hectic and focused on getting ahead that we forget the importance of working with a parent-teacher group, or coaching a soccer or baseball team. Over time, this all just built up in me. Seeing the value in that was far more important. There's no joy in dying and saying you had $20 million. Big deal, who cares?! It's how you spend your life that's important, not what you left behind.

You've taken what many would judge to be a very risky step, and you're still in the early stages. What kind of doubts have you had about your choice, or have you felt centered and on course since the decision?

PAT: I'm reasonably calm, but I wouldn't say we're on course because we don't have a clue where we're going with this! Part of it, this comes from Jean, is if you know what you want to do, you need to have a little faith you can do it, then just go and do it. Take off and see what happens. This isn't do or die— we do have rental property to back us up.

We'll take it one step at a time. We'll try and get connected with the right people and see what comes out of it all. I'm sure it will take some time.

Jean, you left the company a year before your husband, but for similar reasons. What has the past year been like for you? What do you miss and not miss about the entrepreneurial way of life?

JEAN: That was a huge change. I worked there since we started the company. It was a big decision. A lot of the decision was based on the trip to Africa, a realization that the business wasn't everything, there were other options to pursue. I had never really felt like that before. You get head down into what you're doing, carried away by deadlines and projects, and you go from one to the other without thinking, "Is this what I'll do for the rest of my life?" The trip to Africa made me realize there's a whole other world out there.

That seems to be happening with more and more people.

JEAN: You get out of the box and realize, "Oh, there's more to life than what I'm doing. There are all these people over here with nothing who are enjoying their lives." There *are* other ways to live your life.

Before you made the trip, did you have a growing feeling that something was lacking?

JEAN: I had a degree in home economics and later a degree in data processing. So in the back of my mind, I always wanted to do more creative things. I love to sew and to make window treatments, and I had no time for that. I started out part-time when the children were young, and as the years went on I just worked more and more. I had no time for other hobbies and interests.

So many people never get to the point of acting on that.

JEAN: The trip was the catalyst.

But you had to make the decision to make the trip.

JEAN: Pat made that decision! I had never thought about going to Africa, and I didn't want to make the trip at first. But I went along, thought maybe this was something neat, and then I got caught up in it.

Do you remember a certain moment when it felt right, or did it just grow on you?

JEAN: From the time I got there, everything was so completely different, their whole culture. It was really a bombardment of your senses, in every direction. There were several instances when the children would dance at nighttime programs, and I'd see their mothers standing around, watching their children perform. I thought, "That could be up the road here (in Lexington) at school, where I watched our kids in talent shows. These people aren't any different." It just opened things up.

You both have referred to this not being a huge risk for you financially, but it's a big psychological leap, isn't it?

JEAN: With our own business, I had depended a lot on Pat's decisions about the direction I was going to take. When I quit, then I was depending on myself, which was nice.

Pat and I were so involved in the business, we'd come home at night and talk about it all week. It was 18 hours a day. We'd sit down to relax, and I don't know how many times we'd say, "Okay, we're not going to talk about it any more tonight," but within five minutes it would come up again. I thought, "This is crazy. Why should life be like this?" Since I had been thinking about doing other things, I was the one who opted to take the plunge.

We think most people at some level probably yearn to do the same kind of thing you're doing.

PAT: My job was a very stressful job. You get to the point where you have to ask, "Do you want to enjoy life or not?" People work all their lives, get to 65 and retire and think they'll enjoy life, and they really don't. Ideally, you ought to be able work for 20 years or so, then take off at 45 or 50 and go do what you'd like to do, then go back and work some more. But very few people have the chance to do that.

You talked about the rat race and being consumed by your business. What happens if you get caught up working 18 hours a day with this project to sell the villagers' crafts?

PAT: I'm not going to do that this time. My definition of involvement at this point is to be into five or 10 different things, all on the periphery, and let other people spearhead and drive them. I won't let it consume my life, but I'll help find the resources and the people who are willing to let it consume their lives.

Jean, what lessons have you been able to already impart to Pat as he goes through the same process you did a year ago?

JEAN: First, you have to have the space to work. Our first problem was, we didn't have our spaces set up. Then you have to have a schedule. If you don't you could end up lying in bed all day and do nothing. I get up at the same time and have a set schedule every day, with goals to reach.

Since making your decision, do you find that things come easier? Do you feel more creative, more excited about things?

PAT: I sleep better. I get up earlier.

JEAN: He smiles a lot more.

Your lives are definitely changing in a major way. Was there another point in your lives when you reached a moment of truth? What was that experience like?

PAT: When we went into business for ourselves, that was a major change. In hindsight, it was very good. In the beginning, going from employed to self-employed, it forced me to work a lot more hours, for fear that the work wouldn't be there down the road. I spent a lot more time away from home, and had less time to focus on my family.

In one respect, it helped us when Brian was 9 and 10 years old and got involved in soccer. It helped us operate as a family. We traveled a lot to tournaments together. It gave us the opportunity to get together as family. That was a plus, a defining moment.

But clearly, the single biggest impact in our whole lives was our trip to Africa in 1997. The specific moment was the time we made our initial $100 contribution to the church. Twenty-five women from the church came down to thank us. They all brought us gifts: eggs, sugar cane, oranges, a few tomatoes. These people have virtually nothing. That was probably the deciding moment for me. You don't realize it at the time, but when we got back and thought about the whole African experience, that was the moment in time we always remembered. We woke up and said, "We are going to build that church." We knew it was because of that.

That was also where I realized I got the most enjoyment out of life in doing things like that. I realized it was time to focus on that, then, instead of going to work every day. We've been very fortunate, we're in a position that will allow us to do those kinds of things. And we'll do them, too.

You two probably don't regard yourselves as "leaders," but when you're living in sync with your values, that's exactly what you're doing—leading.

PAT: I think if you can share your positive experiences, and people feel good about them and do something like it, that's good.

From your description of Ghana and its citizens, they seem to have a well-developed sense of the "precious present," whether they're seizing opportunities or showing gratitude. How has seeing that enhanced your own sense of appreciation and wonder?

JEAN: You think more about your personal relationships. I find myself thinking, "If those people in Africa were here, how would they look at this?" It changes the way you look at things.

PAT: I think our relationship has been strengthened a lot. We're a lot more in tune with each other. I try to be more in tune to Jean and to enjoying life together. I sold the business and we took a trip and really enjoyed ourselves. I'm just a lot more relaxed in general.

JEAN: We have more time and less stress. We've developed and redeveloped some friendships, because we can see our friends more than we used to.

PAT: The other side is, it's helped me accept things more the way they are. It's hard to complain about getting a little water in your basement when you see open sewers throughout an entire country.

What's the biggest thing that keeps people from pursuing their dreams?

JEAN: Fear of the unknown.

PAT: Fear, and an unwillingness to take that first step. Most of us just procrastinate and wish and dream. We've done it thousands of times ourselves. It isn't like we've pursued every dream that ever came about.

What advice do you have for people who have suffocated or held back their own dreams? What's the first step toward changing where they're at?

PAT: You've got to have the confidence you can do it. Then you just go try it. If you have skills, motivation and desire, you can always do something. If it doesn't work, you can try something else. It's not like life's over.

JEAN: I think you need to look ahead, see where you want to be when you retire, and if you aren't headed there, you need to do something about it.

PAT: Tom Peters talks about having passion, and having that will help you get things done. There's a lot of truth to that, whether it's growing a beautiful garden or working or helping people. If you have a passion for it, you'll find a way to get it done.

People seem to be regaining that sense of passion. But why do you think we lose touch with that in the first place?

PAT: People are caught up in getting ahead, being better off than the Joneses. It's materially and financially driven. We're driven by having to have money for things. You work longer and harder and sacrifice. Eventually you realize you either have it or you don't need it. Some people think you have to have a Mercedes or a 5,000-square foot house or a trip to Florida. They strive and work themselves to death so they can do that. Then they spend that vacation on the beach on their cell phones talking to the office five times a day. What kind of a vacation is that?

I'd be content to go down to the end of the road here and sit in a trailer in the woods for two or three days if that's all I could afford, if I had the peace and quiet. But we get so hung up in this materialistic world.

People seem to be realizing that the rat race isn't so great.

PAT: You're right, the quality of life issues are more important to people now than just getting ahead, sacrificing, doing a job you hate because it pays good money. You see that there's not so much loyalty to employers anymore, which is the employ-ers' fault, not the employees' fault.

JEAN: People change jobs so much more than they used to. You used to start a job and hope to be there for the rest of your life. There are more opportunities to make those decisions at each juncture in your life.

Could you have had the perspective you have now 20 years ago?

JEAN: No, and I don't think you tend to do that when you're younger. You like the idea of a career, and you should. But after a while, it gets old.

PAT: I don't know when one makes this decision, but when you realize that you have enough financial means, to where you're not worried about paying the bills, once you reconcile that to yourself, it opens the door to the question "What do you want to do now?"

What about the genesis of your dream? For instance, the Africa trip didn't happen because you wanted to make a lifestyle change. Was it more instinctual? Did things just begin to snowball?

PAT: For me at first it was just a getaway, a chance to take some time, go and do something, and give a little back. For me, there were never any intentions beyond that. Not until three or four months after we got back did I have this sense of wanting to return and do more.

What happened?

PAT: It's humbling. The people are certainly wonderful. You go from a high tech, instant access world to a village with no running water, no electricity. They have their family and re-ligious values, and that's what they live on. That's more than we have in a lot of respects. They're not into one-upping people and getting ahead. Instead, life is simple. The kids come out and play when the moon is full.

JEAN: The church gave us a direction to take, too. When they showed us their church falling apart, that gave us a direction to go if we wanted to take it. We talked to our pastor about raising funds to rebuild that church. When he gave us the go-ahead, that started the ball rolling.

PAT: There's that passion again. It was real clear to us that we were going to build that church somehow, even if our church wasn't going to be able to back us up. It didn't seem right that people with such strong religious values had no place to go to church. Here we have this multimillion dollar cathedral where some people go only because it's their Sunday obligation. It's hard to sit there and rationalize that they don't have a church and will never get it unless somebody helps them, while we walk in up here and have everything. It was pretty simple for me.

What role did faith have in this decision?

PAT: I'm sure it has a lot to do with it. Our project to Africa was centered around Christ the King Church. Habitat is certainly a Christian organization. And of course the outcome of the Habitat work was deciding to build the church. Outreach ministries at the church are strong now, with 17 subcommittees all helping people in other organizations. Our ties to the church have gotten a lot stronger the last couple of years—from just going on Sunday to being actively involved in things that go on there.

Doing this work has drawn us closer to our faith, given us a lot more trust in ourselves to get done what we want to do. There's no formula or grand plan. Through our faith, we think it will somehow happen.

Pursuing dreams seems to first involve the courage to take a risk.

PAT: I think finding that willingness is your faith coming out in you. I don't have a clue how it's going to work. But if it's important and the right thing to do, somehow it will happen.

David Lyman: His dream of workshops and a college centered on creativity has turned into a mecca for thousands of people.

7

DAVID LYMAN
SAILOR, ENTREPRENEUR,
"VIEW FINDER"

*"I love the dreaming of what is possible.
There are so many things we can do."*

Take a drive up Route 1 into Maine, and eventually you'll make a quick turn down a hill toward the Atlantic Ocean and the picturesque village of Rockport. Surrounded by historic dwellings with spectacular views, decorated with masts and rigging of all shapes, sizes and points of origin, the harbor at Rockport is probably the most photographed in the world. And perched just above that harbor are some of the world's best image makers.

Since 1973, Maine Photographic Workshops has been an international center for the world's photographers, filmmakers, digital artists and writers. It's also been the life's work of its founder, director and "view finder," David Lyman—who, in the words of none other than David Lyman, "has been dumb enough to not know he could do it, but who was wise enough to listen to what others advised."

That sort of irreverent humor and candor—even when he's applying it to himself—is David's hallmark. So is Maine Photographic Workshops, where more than 250 one-week workshops, master classes and three-month professional courses are offered. In addition, David's school offers two-year college degrees in photography, film, video and digital media.

Officially recognized as Rockport College, this creative mecca continues to grow and evolve, the latest addition being a $1.5 million, 30-room hotel for students. Special programs are offered in such places as Tuscany, Provence, Sarajevo, Peru, the Caribbean Islands, Oaxaca, Mexico and, now, Cuba.

Every Monday morning during summer workshop season, newly arrived students file into Union Hall to hear David deliver his near-legendary talk on creativity. Just as the harbor has protected vessels for hundreds of years, David strives to shelter and nurture the creative soul in this fine art enclave. On this particular Monday, as the sun burns off the morning fog, David's energy clears the cobwebs, preparing the way for a week or two of intense artistic work in an intensely beautiful setting. The room is quiet, yet bubbling with expectation. Everyone is eager to get down to work.

David has spent half his life cultivating that atmosphere. He describes the Workshops as "an alternative to traditional academic education, a place where creative artists and image-makers meet to explore their intuition, master their craft and enlighten their vision." A native New Englander, David comes from a family of musicians. But after struggling to master an instrument, David says that his father let him off the hook.

"My father said, 'I hereby absolve you of having to play that instrument any more,'" he tells his workshop audience with a smile. "I discovered my instrument was a tape recorder, making music, but with the talents of others. I managed a coffee house in Boston during the urban folk revival. I produced a dozen albums. I was the first to pay Carly Simon and James Taylor to sing. I loved being around the musicians, but I couldn't do it myself. But I found something they didn't have. I could put together and promote concerts."

Since then, David has worked as a photojournalist in Vietnam, built night clubs and founded arts festivals. He has been a top caliber downhill skier, and also covered world class skiers as a photographer. He has sailed solo offshore between his home in Maine and the Caribbean. He even invented a solar still. But his one constant drive is to help others discover their creative and professional potential—through his own teaching and the community of artists he brings together at the Workshops.

"I was almost bankrupt at one point," he says of the early days, "but I found out the Field of Dreams truth: Build it and they will come."

The rest, as they say, is history. In discovering a career where he gets to stir his dreams and activate them in others, David explored other avenues that, while not dead ends, were not his true calling.

"My mother thought she was going to be a dancer, but at 62 she realized she made a much better mother than she ever would have been a dancer," he says. "When I heard that, I realized that my career as a photographer might not be my calling, that building a school for other photographers might be what I was cut out for."

As a lightning rod for creativity, however, he's tops. David has written and lectured widely on the creative process and helped many to renew their creative lives. In one of his courses, "Discover Your Creative Potential," he incorporates daily exercises in energy management, self esteem, goal setting, journal writing, and the important processes of day and night dreaming. It's all designed to recharge and renew people of all walks of life, whether they be painters, CPAs or both. Some leave the intense workshop experience utterly changed, headed in dramatic new directions with their relationships, careers and artistic vision. Most make less dramatic but no less powerful modifications. They find ways to dovetail their artistic and creative work into their suddenly not-so-run-of-the-mill work lives.

"According to the Myers-Briggs test, creative types are I/E, N, F, P. What is interesting is that only five percent of people in the country are this type and have a creative temperament," he reminds his audience. "Since most people are S, T, Js—the direct opposite of N, F, Ps—most of the world thinks that we creative people are strange. But the world hires us to be innovative. They hire us to tell stories, look inward, invent things that they need. If they could understand us better, they might give us more freedom to do what we do best. One thing creative people are blessed with is curiosity. Creative people don't mind getting lost. We don't have to have an answer. We love the process of searching, discovering."

David has been no less a searcher in his personal life. Only recently, at age 60, did he become a father for the first time with his significant other, Julie Robinson. The child's name? Renaissance. As in rebirth, as in new beginnings—something David has been cultivating all his life, with all its inherent risks.

"I'll tell you what risk is: being close to 60 and starting a family," he says, laughing. "And I thought sailing across the Atlantic was risky."

He and Julie have had to postpone a "round the world" sailing attempt. But like all risks—including this latest one of fatherhood—David is finding that the reward is great. For him it's like doing good work, the kind of engrossing process that not only consumes an artist but takes him or her outside boundaries—where untested fears and uncharted waters can be faced.

"In sailing," he once wrote in *Training & Development Journal,* "I have found that if I fix a position on the chart based on insufficient information, and then draw a course from that supposed position, I stand a much better chance of steering into disaster than if I wait until I am closer to my destination and more accurate information is available."

In other words, truly creative work, like sailing, takes place in the here and now, receiving and acting on information as you go. You can have all the gadgets and maps at the ready, but the essence of discovery is what you do outside the plan—and outside yourself.

"The idea is not you," he counsels the workshop artists before him. "The ego can get in the way. Like our children, our ideas don't belong to us. They are merely in our custody for a while. Ask yourself this: Would you be willing for the work to be seen without your name attached to it? If not, your ego is in the way."

At the same time, he knows the risks associated with such thoroughly exhausting work. And he consciously leads his students through the minefield of fears that hold them back.

"Some people become so traumatized by failure that they don't try anything again," he says. "Between boredom and anxiety is an area called 'Flow.' And between flow and anxiety is The Edge, where you feel uncomfortable, a bit out of your element."

The Edge is where learning takes place. As James Gleick has written in his monumental book *Chaos*, "At the edge, life blossoms." For David, this is the place of personal transformation. "One of the things that stops people from really living is being off the learning curve," he says of this special zone. "But being on it can lead to burnout, I have to warn you."

For David, it's all about the stretch, which he considers the perfect metaphor for growth and discovery. We can operate on a certain plateau for a time, but the urge to improve and to learn more—to do something different that will deepen us as dreamers and as human beings—is not only something that can distinguish an artist, but also unite a team or ignite an organization to a new sense of mission.

"I hope you have a great, creative life," he tells the roomful of students. "Let's go to work."

A CONVERSATION WITH DAVID LYMAN . . .

What do you believe are the absolute keys to success— whether it's a career, a creative endeavor or, as you help people discover, both at once?

I think it has to do completely with attitude, not talent or experience. You hear some people who come here say that the film industry is dead, while others say it's crazy because there's so much work.

I tell my students that there are five keys to success. The first is persistence. Plan on taking at least 10 years to really master your craft. In jazz they say it's a process of imitation, then assimilation, then innovation. In the first two years, if you're not a dilettante, you learn 70 percent of the craft, but it takes the next eight years to master another 20 percent. Then there's the quality of idea, the aesthetics. Usually, after about four years of immersion your aesthetic sense leaps. Persistence is also about discipline—doing what you know you need to do, even when you don't like doing it. There are a lot of things pulling us down, and there's a lot of negativism to battle out there.

The second key is being nice to work with, being a positive and enthusiastic person. We train most of the camera assistants in the film industry now. They're probably the most important person on the film set, because they're enthusiastic about being able to fix something. I'll always hire somebody who's enthusiastic over somebody who knows something. Experts can become a pain in the ass to deal with. Our job is to re-motivate them, to see if the work they're doing is in line with their value system.

The next key is who you know. You need good teachers and coaches. Arthur Rubinstein, even at age 92, had a piano teacher. And you need your peers. We go through a lot of effort at the Workshops through portfolios and prerequisites to assemble equal peer groups. Next, you need to master your craft. What is that valuable thing you know how to do? What skills have you polished, and how are you constantly honing that mastery?

Finally, you need the talent, the natural ability to do something. We're all made differently. And an interest in something doesn't mean you'll have talent. At the same time, I've found that people who have a modicum of talent, and have to work at it, will have a much higher success rate than those who seem to have a lot of talent but little drive to use it.

Can you describe some practical ways for people to develop these attributes?

First, work for yourself. The problem with working for somebody else is the caution. Find something you can screw up and no one cares. Photographers should be doing 72 exposures a week. What do actors do? They drive cabs and wait tables. Every customer is a performance.

Everybody needs a wall, too. A wall devoted to your projects. You stick stuff up on it—photographs, quotes, words. Fill that wall with work and eventually the wall will start talking to you. The work will start to tell you where your weaknesses and strengths are. After a year, those images that stay on the wall will reveal a sequence, a pattern.

This work is not an intellectual process. It can only happen by looking back at what you've done. The work between the pictures you're thinking about becomes more important. I'll guarantee you, the work that's the best will be the work you haven't thought about.

I also think you have to keep a journal. It's cheaper than therapy. Read Edward Weston's daybooks, for instance. Learn to do proprioceptive writing. You sit down and write automatically at first. What the weather is like, what you had for breakfast ... then, before you know it you're writing things down you had no intention of writing.

How do you work with people to overcome fears that hold them back from pursuing a special dream or project?

There's a battle between fear and enthusiasm, between paralysis and going off unprepared. Our job at the Workshops is to help people overcome the fear. Ralph Rosenblum was a very successful film editor for many years, and he always threw up the first day of the job, even on his last big film. He said, "The fear has always been with me. I just haven't allowed it to stop me."

I believe you're either born an optimist or a pessimist. Some pessimists can be made less pessimistic, but never turned into optimists. On the other hand, optimists can never be made into pessimists, though we can be made into cynics.

I ask people to sit down and list why they're afraid, then list the consequences. There are about 50 fears, including the fear of success. But you can overcome that fear by doing a few simple things. First, get the tools you'll need for your project and learn how to use them. Then, go find a teacher, a mentor. Find the experts, too, who have mastered their craft. Next, be sure to take small steps. And finally, as we make certain at the Workshops, do it with a peer group, which provides both great feedback and a safety net.

You draw from a wide variety of sources in your work on the creative process and personal motivation. How do you bring it all together?

All the motivational speakers are saying exactly the same thing, just from slightly different points of view. It's just like the Gospel. It's been the same for hundreds of years, and the only reason it makes an impression is that the original writers, and then the priests and preachers, retell it with new passion and conviction. This stuff is the same way, and motivational speakers have a similar calling to do it. They like going out and sharing it. I enjoy it every morning.

That "gospel" of motivation and discovery involves dreams as well. How do we make dreams real?

Dreams float around in the atmosphere, and they land on people like spores or seeds. Sometimes they land on the sidewalk, or in the cracks in the sidewalk, where they can't grow. And sometimes they land on a fertile piece of ground and they become huge oak trees. Ideas fall on all kinds of people. There are people before me and after me who have had ideas like the Workshops, but they didn't pick the right place, they didn't have the right combination of personalities. Maybe their ego was too involved. Or their pocketbook was either too involved or not enough.

Money is a motivating factor. My printer has a sign in his shop that says, "We can deliver quality, price and speed—pick any two." Likewise, I will do something either because it makes me feel good, it makes other people feel good, or I can make a lot of money—pick any two.

It's a delicate combination, that pocketbook stuff. If you think too much about the money, that's all you'll think about. If you have that non-profit attitude where you don't think about it enough, you'll go belly up anyway, because you're not paying attention to business. I happen to have trod that line, partially through ignorance, and so far we've made it. We're still riding the edge. That building over there, for $1.3 million, is a huge financial undertaking. We didn't have a contract on it until it was already being built.

Do you call that riding your edge?

After you've done this for a while, after you've done business like this or sailed single-handed across the ocean, it's not a risk anymore. You know you have enough options, enough other things, enough redundancy that you can say, "I can handle this." It is still a risk, but it's one you're prepared to take.

A lot of people take risks they're not prepared to take. They're fools. Sometimes the fools make it. Sometimes the guy who's brilliantly experienced tries the same risk and fails, because something just happens.

But more often, would you say people are hampered by their fears instead of their foolishness?

Ninety-five percent of people are too timid. If they do have an idea, they don't have enough passion for it. They're afraid of the passion that they have inside of them.

I fail at a few things every year. And I piss people off and lose money. Does it stop me from doing these things? No. I can't. I found many years ago that momentum is an extremely important part of this whole business. You just keep going. Persistence. If you get going, if you just keep moving, it's going to take a lot to stop you. Now that can be good or bad, because you could be headed in the wrong direction. But if you think and feel that what you're doing is right, then you're probably headed in the right direction. Good decisions and judgments are made when the left and right brain are working together.

Most people don't even start. They talk a lot about it—they talk and talk and talk about it. There is a harbor in Beaufort, North Carolina, that's the last jumping off spot to the Caribbean. It's 1,200 miles from that point. That harbor is full of people who have been there for years, waiting to leave. "I'm waiting for a new part to the engine." "Uh, the weather's not good today." "I just lost my crew and I'm waiting for some more friends to come." It's the generator, or the sails.

There's an old adage I learned in gymnastics. When you're on a piece of apparatus, bounce, bounce, bounce and do it. You can bounce once or twice or thrice, but after three, you won't do it. Not only that, but all that bouncing is taking up a lot of energy. And your chance of success is greatly diminished, the more you hesitate. So the old observations that Tom Peters came up with in *In Search of Excellence*—the importance of passion and attention to detail—are true.

People have been learning to make great pictures here for more than a quarter century now. Let's talk about how this place has grown. How did such a dream begin, and how does it evolve?

Yesterday, John Davis, who just retired from the construction business, pulled up in front of my new building, and he asked me, "Did you ever think when you started this place that you'd be building something this big?"

I said no. It got me thinking about the dream of building something, any idea. What I had to begin with was that this would be very successful if I could get a few *National Geographic* and *Life* photographers together here for a week and I could learn from them. Then I realized that we could add fine art and a few other things to it. Then the third year I thought, "We could add cinematography to this." The process of organizing and marketing and thinking about what else I could do became an enjoyable process. I still get a huge buzz over that.

I have a huge buzz right now over Cuba. We have just been licensed by the U.S. Treasury Department to offer educational programs in Cuba, and bring Americans over legally. We've been working on that for over a year. I've been thinking already. If we can do this, I figure we can do 13 or 14 workshops down there this winter. What can we do? We have to do some travel stuff, some photojournalism, some craft, video, writing . . . . I'm glowing now because I have something to work on. As far as the execution goes, I'd just as soon hire somebody else to take care of the details.

It was not in my dreams to start a college, to grow this big. I dreamt small dreams every year about what this place could be like the following year. I still can't see five or 10 years down the road. Staff members ask me, and I just say, "Let's get better at what we're doing."

A mission statement is very important. Going through that process, as a company or an individual, means finding out what you stand for. I didn't have to do that until we became a college. But I enjoyed that process. It was a huge growth curve for me and for the school, to go through the process that the state was forcing me through. It involved about ten pounds of paperwork, and a two-day visit by other college presidents.

One of the things they said we had to do was write a mission statement. I said, "Look at the catalog," and they said, "Well, yes, there is a lot of writing there, but it doesn't say anywhere what you are."

So I said, "Well, that's kind of interesting, because everybody comes here for a different reason. I don't want to say what I think it is, because people have been defining it for themselves for years." So I was reluctant. But then one day I was in the Caribbean on the boat, and I put down two words together: image-makers and storytellers. That's what we are at the Workshops. If you can write a mission statement that is one sentence, that says "We are a conservatory for the world's storytellers and image-makers," that defines who we are.

Then we have to see what we need to do to fulfill that. We're not offering any courses in storytelling or performance. How important is anthropology and myth? So now, what we do reflects that mission.

Where do you begin with such seemingly huge undertakings as the Workshops, which in turn led you to create a college?

Every time I start something, it usually starts on the back of an envelope or on a shirt cardboard. Sometimes they come in the middle of the night. "OK—a workshop, with 15 people, at $1,000 a person—that's $15,000. Hey, I can make a killing on this!" That is indeed another aspect of motivation, enough to make you say "OK, I think I could do this." Now very seldom do you make the amount of money you envision, but just the fact that you thought you could moves you farther ahead. Then you see what other things it will take.

That little list, I keep telling everybody, is important. It's partly intellectual, and it's partly listening to your inner self. "What am I afraid of?" "What am I not going to do that I will kick myself later for not having done?" If you put those things down—the news release, the ad, the poster—those are the things that I've realized over the years add up to success. If you gain enough experience, the success rate gets higher. Then the big problem becomes keeping it fresh and alive so it doesn't become boring.

Cuba keeps me fresh right now. Cuba was impossible. But through a lot of persistence and letter writing and talking to my senator and having her write letters and calling up the Treasury Department and more letters, it's done! Now we'll have a workshop in Cuba. We're doing a Hemingway short story workshop at the Hemingway home near Havana, with a Hemingway scholar and a top mystery writer named Robert Butler.

I love the dreaming of what is possible. There are so many things we can do.

It's interesting what you say about making planner lists: "Make a list of what you must do. Then make a second list of the two things you must do that day. Do those two things, forget the rest."

You have to think of what will move you forward. If you try to do a dozen things, you get conflicted with the goals. We put a lot of busywork in the way. Some of us don't like to address those major issues. But those major issues are important. They possess us, and we're often afraid of that possession, because we know the effort it's going to take, and we know it's going to change our lives. We may not want our lives to change. That's one of the things that can lead to failure. It's also a fear of success, however.

How is it that projects can start with one dimension, but turn into more opportunities and uses than had been foreseen?

It's all about process. The process will lead you to discover what's possible. What you initially think is possible is actually very small. It may be so grand that you'll never achieve it because you don't know the first step. But if you're just involved in process, like a photographer making photographs on a daily basis, after you've been doing it for a while, the work you're making will start to tell you what it is you're doing. If you think about what you're going to do first, you won't go through the process of discovery.

Discovery is an important part of innovation, of developing an attitude toward creativity. That's where the joy and the thrill come. If you're not discovering things, why do it anymore?

Over the years, you've found out how the workshop model works in different disciplines. How does it work in an organizational context, say within a company or school? Is there a way to bring a workshop model into your everyday process?

What I've found is that it's about leading an art-full life. Bringing art into your life—or bringing it into your company. That doesn't mean just having an attractive environment with pictures on the wall and good music on the stereo system. An artist is someone who is following an inner path. They are doing things that reflect their inner values. They're listening to that part of them that is not ego, not intellect, not emotions, but intuition.

The way I look at it is that we put on intellectual, ego, and emotional faces in our daily lives. The intellect is the ability to be witty, to use the language, to tell jokes, to negotiate and schmooze. But it's surface, it's a mask.

The real deep inner stuff comes from looking at what you have done. If you haven't done enough stuff that's personal, or reflects your inner artist or inner values, there's nothing to look at, nothing to mark where you've been. A lot of people come to this place in their thirties and forties and say "I want to be a photographer," "I want to be a filmmaker," "I want to be a writer—please teach me."

Well, we can help. But you're not going to make a lateral shift just like that. You're going to go way down and become a failure at what you're doing until you go through all the processes to be good at it.

I think it is a spiritual pathway that the CEO or the owner of a company needs to take. He or she needs to go someplace and be quiet for a while and read some stuff, and become very much in touch, very clear and clean. I think every company, and every company leader, needs to do that.

And how do you then blend the creativity of so many individuals?

Look at a symphony orchestra or a film crew. A symphony orchestra piece has only one composer, then 80 people in the orchestra itself, then one conductor. I was on the set of *On Golden Pond* for several weeks doing a series of magazine articles. There was one author of the screenplay, one director, and a cast and crew of 80—just like an orchestra!

Most of the people in the world are doers. They love working the camera, doing the makeup, editing, playing the cello or trumpet. But most of them don't have the personality to be solo musicians. They like to be part of the group. It takes a special quality to be a soloist. Most of them probably could—they just prefer not to.

They are great at playing individual notes, but they need someone to bring perspective to those notes. "I want the string section to sing. I want the brass section to lower the volume." It brings perspective to the individual notes.

The commercial world is the same as the creative world in this respect. You have a whole factory building stuff. Do they know who their audience is? Do they know who they're building for? Do they know the importance of their job within this whole thing? Even if their job is to put one nut on one bolt.

You give great priority to the importance of time for reflection and meditation. Isn't that becoming increasingly hard to do? To some people, just half an hour seems hard to come by.

First, I don't think that they know. If we could tell them, "Look, this is what can happen in a whole day, and this can transpire in a three-day weekend. In one week, this will happen. If you take a sabbatical for three or four months, this is what might happen."

The focus today is on the structures by which change can be affected in a culture or group. So you take everybody off on a two-day retreat. Well, that's mostly entertainment. No real change is made. No one in the organization shifts their paradigm.

It's just a lot of group meals.

Yes, and a little bonding, some jokes. They're sort of forced through this stuff, because they didn't really want to go anyway.

We just had a three-day workshop with Matt Mahurin. I have talked to two of the top photographers in it and they say they were profoundly affected. Normally that takes a week, at least, to make a full change, a full realization. But I think the people who went through those three days, if it had been a week, would have said it couldn't be one day shorter. Everybody is asking for more time, nobody is asking for less.

It's like a vacation. Most people go on a one-week vacation. Sunday you leave home and arrive. Monday you're getting settled and finding out where everything is. Tuesday you explore around the village or town. By Wednesday, you finally get to the pool or the beach with your book and your friend and you lie down and say "Aah, this is it." Two hours later, it's time to confirm reservations, and tomorrow you need to do the souvenir shopping for the kids. Your vacation was two hours long!

Trying to shed all the baggage takes two days. And then there's anticipation. Myself, when I go off for a month on the boat, the last couple days before I come back, my mind is totally focused on what I have to do when I get home. So I think a vacation has to be two weeks minimum. Those first and last three days will still be the same, but you can stretch that period in between.

Now some people will say, "Oh, I try to grab a little each day."

That doesn't work. It works in a certain regard. I try to grab a little each day myself. But we're talking about a vacation where you can restore yourself spiritually, physically, emotionally. You have to rest, to flush out your system. There are times when I'm so stressed out that I can't think straight. And I have two things to finish and get into the mail by five. So I go lie down, right in the middle of everything hitting the fan. Because I know from experience that if I can just get 10 minutes of quiet, the whole stress reduces. It's a physical thing that happens. One of the meditations people use is looking at the stress in your system as a viscous substance like motor oil, which you are going to drain out of your system. Before you know it, you're gone. It takes about eight and a half minutes for that chemical change to happen in your body.

You do have control. You can do something to change things, to affect the process.

What have you given up to pursue your dream at the Workshops? How difficult was it to do so?

That's an interesting question, because I often talk about sacrifice being part of the process. I gave up not having a stable relationship until the past five years. I never really had a stable one, though my relationship with a woman named Kate, who later died in a car crash, was the most profound. I gave up having children until I was 60. I gave up security, which I never really looked at as being important anyway. Fame as a photographer or a writer. But look at the consequences of what I've done. I started a college, which very few people have done in their

I started a college, which very few people have done in their lives. I own a college, which nobody does. It's a unique institution based on a unique philosophy that's keeping alive intuition—the world of an artist. So, was it a sacrifice at all, or was it just choices I made?

Certainly there are sacrifices along the way. Relationships died along the way because I didn't spend the time I needed to with that person. My career as a photographer went on the back burner 20 years ago; books I have wanted to write. I haven't done any of the writing I've wanted to do because this place needs me right now, it needs my energy. Is that more important than writing the books? It's like a bird in the hand is worth two in the bush. I have the Workshops, and I know what that is, and I don't want to do anything to jeopardize it. I don't want to just turn my back on this to write the books, because the message given here is the same as in the books.

What's interesting is that a workshop is 10 times more profound than any book. It's a physical, human experience you go through. A book is someone else's experience you read about. It's vicarious. With a workshop, you're guaranteed to have a more profound experience. You will move somebody or be moved. The connection is so strong. That to me is a great calling in life. To have done that, over and over again.

For some people it is a sacrifice. They give up a job, a lifestyle. I often tell people, "Look, one of the reasons you're not going anywhere is you're not ready to give up something." They're not ready to give up the lifestyle, the car, the vacation home, the condo. They have to make $150,000 a year or they're not happy. But they could get by on a lot less and still be happy—maybe happier. Most people who do something they feel is important do it for less money. They could have made more elsewhere.

There's a marvelous illustration of this from Rilke's book *Letters to a Young Poet.* The young man asks, "How do I know that I'm supposed to write?" and Rilke writes back, "Some night, you must ask yourself, 'Would I die if I couldn't write?'" If the answer comes back "yes," then the rest is easy.

You warn that trying to find shortcuts in the creative process is a dead end. How do you communicate this in an era where speed is king?

It has to do with impatience. The photographer Ernst Haas calls photographers "painters in a hurry." We're impatient. I'm basically an impatient person. I want things to happen faster than they're really supposed to happen. So I'm an expert in seeing it in other people, especially the high school kids. "It can't be this hard," they say. "There has to be a secret. What's the right combination?" Well, it *is* this hard, and it should be this hard. It separates out the people who don't have the patience, the discipline, the persistence and determination. Because only those people who are really good are going to be the storytellers, the innovators, the inventors, the people who are going to lead this society.

"Spike Lee made his first feature at age 22," they say. I say, "That's Spike Lee, that's not you." Spike Lee made it not *because* of any school he went to—he made it *despite* every school he had attended. "So, what are you doing here?" I say. "If you're another Spike Lee, go out and do it." There are no secrets. The secret is you have to work hard.

The technology and the advertising for the technology are selling us all short. Most of the hype is by the manufacturers of the hardware and software, not by the people who use it. We're not clamoring for more stuff, we're not asking for faster computers and more software. The stuff we have is fine. We don't need high-definition television. What we have is fine. It's the money people who are driving it. It all has to do with the economy, and nothing to do with the needs of storytellers. People tell me that my computer is out of date and I need a faster one. How much faster? Is it going to add a day to my week? No.

I do think there is a great leap between the typewriter and the word processor. Now that is a technical leap, beneficial to all writers. It made writing a lot easier. But what we find here that's very interesting about the digital world is that we enroll

10 times the number of people in basic darkroom classes as we do in digital classes. People want to *make* pictures. Also, they don't want a workshop on computers—they know they can learn that stuff at home.

Has the fact that we have all these automatic focus and auto exposure cameras made any better photographers? No. It's made for a lot more mediocre pictures in the world. The new tools make things easier for people who already know what they're doing, but it doesn't make the people who don't know what they're doing any better.

Beware of technology. It's an extension of the intellect—it works logically, not intuitively. They try with fuzzy logic to emulate intuition, but it doesn't really work. You see this interactive media stuff people are putting together, and it's so shallow you can actually see the limitations of the creator. The human hand is too heavy in there. Technology services the intellect. And the intellect is too high in our society right now. It's too powerful. It dominates.

Do you find ways to incorporate intuition into the operations of the Workshops?

To become a college and have a real library plan, we had to hire a full time librarian. She was appalled at the disorganization. But I told her I didn't want her to obsess on all this organization stuff. I asked her to maintain a certain degree of haphazardness. Because when somebody goes into a library to find something, they often end up finding something else, which they didn't know about until they got there. So surprises should be built in to libraries. You go in to find one thing, but stumble on something else that's more important. My office is sort of like that, piles all over the place. You kick over something, and it changes your whole day. It's sitting there waiting for you to discover it all this time.

But I couldn't operate the way I do without the organization the computer gives me, because I couldn't find anything. Thank God there's a file finder function.

In some ways, finding that dusty book in the corner of an old library, a book that is not likely to be catalogued on the Internet anytime soon, is a skill that's a competitive advantage.

Stumbling onto things. I think a lot of people at the top end of our industries know that that is a very valuable function—but very few people overall do. Most people embrace the technology, because it gives them that comfort feeling, that things are well in order.

Sailors in the old days sailed a lot by intuition, which is the sum of everything I know. Now there's a GPS system behind you, which cost me 500 bucks. It's the most current form of navigation, all hooked in to the satellites up there. Anywhere in the world I can tell exactly where I am, how fast I'm going, how long it will take me to get someplace, whether I'm drifting one way or another. It's amazing, and it's all intellectual. When you rely on that, your ability to work intuitively becomes diminished, because you're relying on intellectual input rather than all the other things.

The old guys navigated by feelings more than by intellect. Now you read *Sail* magazine, and it's all about how to sail by the little numbers, and the little tweaking. Jeez, people love sailing that way, but it takes all the romance out of it. Then you read *Cruising*, and it's about the food, and where to anchor and how to fix things in storms. One's the scientific way to sail and the other is the more traditional way.

We're losing the intuitive ways of doing things. Artists keep holding on to that. Businesses need to do more of it, and we as individuals need to do more of it. We need to understand that there are more ways inside us, there are more tools we've been given to lead life and solve problems than just the intellect. It's because of our Western society, because of our industrialization, factories, consumerism. Manufacturing, driven by technology, has taken us further and further away. Our educational system today was developed by a team of scholars in Chicago in the early 1800s primarily to train people to work in factories.

The subject matter, memory, rows of desks, calculations—all of it was set up to learn about technology. If you were fortunate enough to be an athlete, or play in the band, you may have learned more about some other aspects of yourself.

I feel that the most valuable class in school, and in which I excelled the most and use today every day of my life, is recess. What did it teach you? Teamwork. Negotiation skills. Leadership. "It's my bat and ball, and you'll play by my rules." It taught you how to talk, how to survive, how not to get beaten up, how to make friends and acquaintances. You may not like the guy, but he has the bat and ball. I like geography, too. And science. But the skills you learn in recess will stand you in good stead the rest of your life.

So how can grown-ups like us invite a little recess into our lives?

People want to incorporate more creativity into their lives. You don't need to become an artist. You just need to do something that's artful. Go to museums. Learn a craft that you can continue to do for the rest of your life. It can be writing, photography, anything. You don't have to do it full-time, but you have to do what you do long enough to master the tools, so that you can access parts of you inside that you don't have access to right now.

Who are you? That's why I talk about the Meyers-Briggs assessment. The people that come here need to know that they're different from the people back home. They can do things in the world that other people can't.

Now a lot of people, when we say we're going to talk about your soul, say, "I leave my soul alone, it leaves me alone. I know people who have gone there and they never came back. No thank you." There is too much of that. The churches often wind up selling that too—"You just do what we tell you to do, and let us take care of your soul."

The problem with that is there's no continued exploration. It's all set up for you. You might as well be dead already. The sermon changes a little bit, but everything else is exactly the same. The joy in life—and what we start as kids and stop when we're 20—is learning what's possible. What else is there to do? "Oh, that's OK, I'm already set for life," somebody will say. "No, you're not," I say back. There's certainly no longer any cradle-to-grave employment. You're going to have to be more risk-oriented, take charge of your own growth, your own profession. "I am a human services resource person, and I do it freelance."

Maybe you'll still work for a company, but as a consultant, not as a paid employee. Now some people have to have those jobs, because they don't have the capacity to handle the freelance world. So our job sometimes is to get these people moved out of the corporations and into the private sector, so they can hire themselves back as consultants. They're going to make more money. The corporation's no longer responsible for them. No more perks. They have to pay them a higher rate, but they don't need them all the time.

That sounds very much like Sally Helgesen's ideas about custom work—customizing your work life to correspond with the rest of your life.

You pick the hours you want to work. If you're a night person, then you don't have to have any morning meetings. Mornings are for your art work, journal writing. You sleep late, because you're going to be working until two in the morning.

You'd probably get along better with colleagues, too.

About half the people who take my creativity class go back to their bosses and ask to reshape the structure of their jobs. "This is what I'd like to do. It's going to cost you less, I'll do better work. See any problem with that?"

How are you going to do that? First, you ask them to guarantee you 150 days of work a year at a set rate. You have another 150 days to do with what you want—work for other people, do your art work, go back to college. All of a sudden your life opens up.

In your case, your dream involves cultivating other people's inner wishes. Tell us about people who have experienced the Workshops as a catalyst for their own dreams.

Many people who took classes here have eventually come back as professionals or instructors in their own right. Men and women meet each other here, get married, have kids. Julie and I met here. We'll bring 2,500 to 2,600 people through here right now. I'd imagine 2,400 of them would say years from now, "That changed me."

People can be affected in all kinds of ways, sometimes profoundly. Some people go home and quit their jobs. Some move, some get divorced. Some will come back to do a three-month or full-year program. Some will simply go back and talk to the people they work with and say, "I need more freedom. I am a creative person, which means I need this kind of stuff to be in my work, and I don't work like you do. I process things differently, yet you need me, because you need somebody in this department that's the creative person, who comes up with the new ideas, who is the storyteller. But I have to work differently. I don't want to come in at eight every morning. You'll get a 40- to 60-hour week out of me, but sometimes I'll need to stay at home."

Of course, the other kind of people don't like that. They like order, structure and regimentation. They like things to be the way they have always been, and they don't like change.

Part of the attraction of the Workshops is that they feed the need for lifelong learning. Does lifelong learning enable lifelong dreaming? What are you learning about right now?

I'm never working on one thing—always five or six things. And most artists are always working on several canvases, most writers on several projects. Cuba is big on my mind right now— what we're going to do down there, the potential. It's something nobody else is doing, so therefore it's very exciting for me. The challenge and the risk is high. I love our programs in Tuscany and Europe, but I'm not as interested as I was before.

There's too much competition, too many people I've spun off. So I figure I'll do something else. I don't have to own the world, after all.

I'm developing an MFA in Cinematography program. A man I talked to said to just make him an offer. It's timely, because he has two films to do in the next year, and it will take me a year to organize it and sell it so we have 20 students in the program when he shows up. I'm excited about working on that.

For me now, that's where the real joy is, exploring things, trying to find out what can happen. In that creative circle diagram I use, I go right up to the model stage, get about halfway through the crafting, and then I say, "I'm bored with this now." I know that well enough about myself. I'm a dreamer and half a doer. So I'm finding more people that are good doers. They can be dreamers, but they shouldn't have too many dreams that compete with mine, because then we have a conflict.

Personally, I have dreams to realize with this boat. We're planning on taking the boat around the world for two years, which is a good excuse for getting the workshops organized. I don't just want to do these things as self-satisfying things. That's masturbation, narcissistic. I want to do them as opportunities to explore, and to share these explorations with other people.

That's certainly an ambitious dream.

See all these houses around this harbor? A lot of them belong to wealthy retirees, who hate the fact there's a college in town. They don't take advantage of it. They just hate the fact that there are people doing things in their little town, people lighting things and flashbulbs going off. It's not a quiet little pre-graveyard. That's what a lot of these little retirement communities are, you know—just one step from the grave. But the guy who lives next to me is the former chairman of the art department at the University of Illinois, Herb Fink. Herb says, "Thank God you're here. I'd have died a lot earlier if there weren't a college in town. It's the young people who keep me alive."

When did you discover that you were not only an artist, but an entrepreneur?

How did that start for me? I'm standing on a ladder at age 14, working in an orchard, picking cherries for 20 cents a quart. I'm lucky to make 80 cents an hour. Some guys make three or four bucks an hour. Also, up this ladder, I can't find anything else to do. If I'm stuck there, working for 20 cents a quart, I can't go out and explore and see if there's something better I should be doing. That's what a job is. It's something you do that you might not even be interested in, that somebody pays you for. They're buying your time.

So when I was 16, my mother said I had to get a job. So I thought about it. This is the beginning of David Lyman's creative life. What could I do that would keep me on the lake? What do people need on the lake that I could charge them money for? Teach sailing? I only had a rowboat. Then the milkman comes to the back door and I thought, "That guy spends all day driving around the lake." What could I do that was like that? How about bread? Pies, cakes, donuts, pastries, loaves of bread.

My mom set me up with the bakery in town. They bankrolled it for the first couple of weeks. I loaded up the rowboat, sold it all before I was halfway around the lake. Finally I had to use the neighbor's boat, towing it behind. I had a bell I would ring at people's docks. They'd come down and buy stuff and order more stuff for next time. You're buying it for 20 cents, selling it for a buck and a half, so there's a huge profit margin. I did fine, and I stayed on the lake all summer long. I was in great shape, I was healthy, I was tan, and only worked three days a week. That was it. I was an entrepreneur. I never worked for anybody else after that.

We always had a plan. The milk man and I would meet on somebody's dock, and sit there with our feet in the water drinking his milk and eating my doughnuts. It seems like cheating, doesn't it? It just wasn't right somehow. We were having way too much fun! It hasn't really changed. I'm doing the same thing now. Except the business has become so big.

How has becoming a father influenced your sense of balance and wholeness? What opportunities does it present to you?

Having a child is a very good lesson for what it is to have an idea. The fact that you don't own it. Your job is to use your best talents and your best energy to help make it real. And that means help. You have to enlist people, because nobody in this world can do it all themselves. No matter how talented you are, you're going to need somebody to sell the idea, package the idea, market the idea, somebody to get the bills out, somebody to craft, somebody to help with the research. You can't do it alone, even though that's what the ego wants.

I now have this daughter, so I have got to be around for her twenty-fifth birthday. So, I'm bound to be here for the Workshops' fiftieth birthday party. If you have those reasons to live, you will live.

There's a joke about an elderly Jewish man who lives in a high-rise condominium on Miami Beach. Every morning he gets into his Cadillac and drives down to the local newspaper building and loads his trunk with newspapers. Then he drives back and sits there in the lobby, selling newspapers to his friends. His buddy Ivan comes by and says, "Moishe, you're a multi-millionaire, you gave the business to the kids, you have all the money in the world. Why are you selling newspapers in the lobby?" Moishe says, "Ivan, if I don't have something to do, He's going to take me."

Somebody asked Jay Maisel at one of his workshops, "What are you doing for a retirement fund?" And he said, "Retirement fund?! I'm a photographer. We don't retire." Being an artist is something you do until the day you die.

Isn't that funny how that has come about? Where did that idea come from? Work for money at a job, then your reward is retirement. Where did that ever come from?

"Get In Touch With Your Dreams" is one of your recommendations. What's the significance of our sleeping dreams?

Sometimes the dreams I have are like watching a great film. And if you don't quickly write them down, they will be totally lost. All you have to write is three or four words. Then you wake up in the morning and read, "Horse. Lake. Bus." And the dream floods back in. The novelist John Gardner said that all you have to do as a writer is write well enough that when you read it, you're back in touch with the fictive dream, with that state of mind that a writer is in when the vision is coming, when the stories and messages and dialogue is coming.

So then you go to your word processor or you sit there on the edge of your bed with your yellow legal pad and you write two pages. Then you put your bathrobe on and sit at your computer and work for four hours. Now it's eight o'clock and you have a meeting at nine and you haven't done anything to get ready for it yet. Why? Because your dream had something to say to you. If we don't do those things, our inner artist withers and dies. We become functionaries, technicians in life, and never become storytellers.

The great priests were supposed to be storytellers. They very seldom are today. They're dogma preachers. And a joke is the foundation for all storytelling. It's a setup and payoff, which is always a surprise. You lead them down the path one way, and then take them back the other way. That is what we're interested in. Often the jokes are *so* bad, but the storyteller is so good that we're interested in the world they create. Good storytellers have those techniques.

Your "Fantasy Life and Career" exercise has much in common with Jack Canfield's belief that recording the specific details of your dreams gets you that much closer to attaining them. Talk about that process.

Daydreams count, too. The problem is, some people think they don't have time to daydream. Or they don't think it's an important part of the process. Some people are paid to do that. If I don't have time to daydream, I don't know where to go next. My job is the vision of this place. What can we do in Cuba? I need to take the time to daydream about that. I'll take some time to cogitate, let the imagination go a little crazy. Then it's time to do the research and the phone calls, but first comes the daydreaming. Some daydream a lot and never do anything. Some don't daydream at all. The person who doesn't daydream is probably a good functionary for someone else's daydreams.

There's a difference between a technician, a craftsman and an artist. A technician is somebody trained on how to use a machine, and they're good at it, but they have no idea what they're making. They can make that piece of metal, but they have no idea where it's going to go. But they can make it perfectly according to the specs. Certain cultures are like that—good at following the rules. The entire society would shut down in Japan and Germany if a traffic light stopped working. Nobody would cross the street.

So do you see America as a land of daydream believers?

Our job is to defy the rules, invent the rules. Our country is founded by a society of outlaws, renegades, ne'er-do-wells. Dissatisfied, ambitious people. Look at who we are as a society. People came because they were dissatisfied with religious persecution back home. Then they come here and are even more strict than back there. We're intolerant. We're adventurers. Those people were so high-risk oriented. They went to a country they had only heard about. Blood curdling stories, where savages cut your scalp off, slit your throat. Who would come over to a country like that? But they came in droves. Why?

Two reasons. First, "I don't like where I am, and so there has to be better than here." Second, opportunity. I think that's what sold most people coming over.

So who are we as Americans? We're still explorers and adventurers. We're also slightly violent, we're definitely technologically-oriented. We had to be, because it was the technology, the guns, that helped us survive. What happened is that America existed in the minds of men thousands of years ago, as a dream. It was a place where they would be with fellow adventurers, fellow explorers, and where they'd be encouraged to succeed. Every other society is negative. In Australia, you're ostracized if you're successful. Europe is the same way.

It happens in America, too, in small towns. My mother was a little that way. She didn't want me to be disappointed, so she didn't want me to strive for too much. I didn't listen at all. After a while she started believing in me and encouraging me. I was her firstborn, after all. Over here, we generally look up to successes. We want to help people succeed.

I've thought about living elsewhere, in the Caribbean, but I couldn't do it. One reason is that Maine is not like the rest of the country. We're more like the people in Nova Scotia and Newfoundland. This is a separate part of the world. We're not like New Hampshire or even Massachusetts—even though it seems like most of the people in Maine are from Massachusetts. I've found a place I can live that feeds the inner me. I love the woods, but I love the ocean, too.

So how is who you are connected with where you live?

I think it goes back to the collective unconscious that Jung talks about, those images you're born with, the symbols that are part of your culture that you don't learn. They're already with you somehow.

It's amazing to watch animals behave in ways they haven't been taught. Or my daughter. She does things and we say, "We didn't teach her how to do that." The instinctual is part of the collective unconscious. It's stuff you're born with. I think about 60 percent of who we are is what we're born with. It happens at the moment of conception. That's the only time that something transfers—bam, that's who you are.

There is a fight now from people who are adopted to find their birth parents. It's because they want to know where they came from. I found two whole shelves in a genealogical library on the Lyman family. I want to write someday about my forefather who came here first, write about what drove him, what he found here. I should be able to write it, because that's what's still so strong in me. I still have that same desire to explore that he had.

Bob Voss: His groundbreaking programs for the mentally retarded have helped many realize an essential American dream—having their own homes.

8

BOB VOSS
ADVOCATE, RISK TAKER,
BOUNDARY BREAKER

"You know there's a chance you'll fall,
but you know what? That's the dignity of risk."

Sometimes, the dreams we dream are not for ourselves. We have dreams for others, particularly those we love—a daughter recently graduated from high school, a close friend embarking on a new career, a newborn grandson with a fresh life in front of him, an aging parent entering what we hope will be a rewarding retirement.

There is also a cadre of unselfish men and women who make the dreams of others their life's work. Among them is Bob Voss.

Bob is a licensed clinical counselor who oversees programs for the mentally retarded in Chardon, Ohio, a small town northeast of Cleveland. Since 1984 he has worked for the Geauga County Board of Mental Retardation and Development Disabilities, and though his role there has changed through the years, Bob's mission has remained the same.

Bob is an irreverent boundary breaker and risk taker. Had he been born 240 years ago instead of 40, he'd

135

probably have been in the midst of the planning for the Revolution. Bob's aim is to make liberty and the pursuit of happiness a reality for the mentally retarded adults and children who are his constituency.

When Bob came to Geauga County, he was just out of Marietta College, one job under his belt. But that job—activity director for the mentally ill—had shown him the value of holistic treatment, of healing people not only through counseling but through art, exercise, music and gardening.

He began talking with mentally retarded adults and learned that while their basic needs were being met, their dreams and desires were going unnoticed.

"We would have 90-day reviews on each individual, and we would talk about their medical condition, their medication, their weight and diet," says Bob. "And I would say, 'OK, now let's get to the good part. What did you do these past 90 days? Where did you go? What did you want to do that you didn't get to do? Why didn't you? Why didn't we follow through?'"

His questions were like a conductor's baton to an orchestra. A symphony of dreams and wishes came pouring out of his clients. They wanted to take a swim, visit the bowling alley, go shopping, take trips. They wanted, in short, to expand their world—the stuff of all good dreamers.

And so it happened that one day Bob and two other staff people loaded up a van with a group of seven middle-aged, mentally retarded men and women who'd never been on a vacation out of the state. They headed out to Washington, D.C. For his clients, it was the journey of a lifetime. For Bob, it was a chance to push the boundaries a bit, to prove to others that, yes, it was feasible to take mentally retarded clients on an overnight trip.

What we love about this story, and what makes Bob cringe even to this day, is that the well-planned trip went awry. Why love that? Well, simply because the experience is an important example of how, though our dreams carry risk, the risk is typically overshadowed by the exhilaration of living our dreams. Remember Jack Nicholson and his boat outing in *One Flew Over the Cuckoo's Nest?* Or Michael Keaton and friends making their escape into the "real" world in *The Dream Team?* Neither of those were placid undertakings, but were they worth it? You bet.

And so it was with Bob's trip. In Washington, on the Mall just outside one of the Smithsonian's museums, Bob and his staff did one of their frequent head counts and came up one short. "We lost Dale at the Smithsonian," he remembers. "It was a whole new learning experience, figuring out how to find a missing person."

Police were called, staff fanned out to look for Dale and, two hours later, he came walking down the street. Because Dale was nonverbal, he couldn't explain where he'd been, but from the cigarette in his hand, the staff surmised he'd gone for a stroll, realizing he couldn't smoke in the museum. The episode could have spelled the end of future road trips, but luckily, Bob's supervisors agreed with him that the trip's value had far exceeded the hazards.

"The good that came out of that trip far outweighed the two hours that we were kind of nervous," Bob says.

Today, trips like that groundbreaking one are commonplace. Meanwhile, Bob has moved into a new role, as community residential services director. In the job, he is literally laying foundations and opening doors for mentally retarded clients to have lives as similar as possible to the rest of the population. He does it by helping them achieve an integral aspect of the American Dream—a place of their own, a home. Through a nonprofit corporation tied to the Geauga board, Bob has been overseeing the purchase of houses for mentally retarded adults since 1992.

The concept is called Supported Living. When it came to Geauga County in 1989, it was a rather new idea throughout the nation. It is still not the norm, but other areas are starting to realize that many mentally retarded people are capable of living nearly on their own and are fashioning similar programs.

Through Supported Living, groups of up to four mentally retarded adults live in homes that blend right in with the rest of the neighborhood. There are eight of these homes in Geauga

County now, with plans for a least one new home in each of the next five years.

Each resident has his or her own room. Although a health care provider does supervise the home, the residents are mostly on their own, often for the first time in their lives. It's a concept that Bob realized was needed after one of his many conversations with some of his clients.

They were talking about where they lived and roommates. Suddenly, one of the clients spoke out. "He told me, 'I hate my roommate. He's a slob. I don't want to live with him anymore,'" Bob says, and he understood exactly the problem. These were 40- and 50-year-old men, living dormitory lifestyles. "Imagine living your whole life with your college roommate," he says.

Bob grew up in a happy, though packed, house, the second of five children. His family was 1950s traditional, with "dad bringing home the bacon and mom frying it," he says. He and his older brother shared a room, so he could nod knowingly when his clients complained about having to share their space.

His father's work in sales led to several moves, but the family was always stable. His mom's chores were nonstop to maintain a seven-member household, and his father sometimes held two to three jobs to provide. Meanwhile, Bob was playing sports, and becoming a very good baseball player. He would, as a high school senior, have an unsuccessful tryout for the Baltimore Orioles, in what he has called one of the most exciting days of his life.

Even on the playing field, he began to exhibit his sensitivity and his tendency to care more about others than about his own success. It showed up particularly when Bob, nearly always a team captain, would pick players for his team. He would pick the worst players, the kids nobody else wanted.

"I always felt like if I was always the last to be picked and was never wanted on the team, I would feel pretty crummy," Bob says. "What I thought was that it would be really neat if, for once, they could be on a winning team and they could feel what it's like to be a winner and not always be a loser. So, if I picked the worst guys and we lost, it was expected. But if we won, oh my God, we had bragging rights."

Home has been a recurring theme of Bob's life, not just in his work but also in his personal life. As his parents' retirement years approached, they built a vacation getaway in the secluded mountains of North Carolina. For Bob, that home came to signify family and closeness. It became the place where parents, children and grandchildren would gather to recharge and reacquaint.

It was another house, a 160-year-old home he and Katie Wheeler have renovated, that ushered in a turbulent time in Bob's otherwise fairly placid and predictable life. In 1993, a tornado swooped through the Fowler's Mill Road neighborhood where the two live. It banged into their sturdy house, uprooted eight large trees in the yard and undid much of the work they had done. Luckily, no one was injured.

For Bob, it was a foundation-shaking experience. "We had put a lot of effort into fixing up this house and restoring it and to have something like that undo everything you've done is a kick in the gut," he says. "It's difficult to have another force outside yourself say, 'Nope, sorry, not going to happen today.'"

He would again be reminded of how quickly life can turn when, not long after the storm, his father was diagnosed with cancer. He died two years later.

"It was another kick in the gut," Bob says. "Everything that happened affected my attitude for a while. I felt that it didn't matter how hard you tried in life because it could all be undone at the snap of a finger."

For the first time, Bob found himself out of what he describes as "the comfortable groove in the middle of the road." For a time, he led a life that he describes as reckless, doing what he wanted to do with little concern about the future because he felt it no longer mattered, that it might all be taken from him, anyway.

After those uncharacteristic few years, normalcy returned. He's plunged into his work for the county's Metzenbaum Supported Living Program, and the future looks bright. A recently approved tax levy will bring more money to the program, which must contend with the high cost of housing in Geauga, one of Ohio's wealthiest counties. At the urging of a supportive board of directors, the program is about to seek new sources for funding, including foundation grants.

At the same time, Bob is dreaming new dreams for the program, the latest being a house designed by an architect to meet the needs of handicapped children. All of his dreams and ideas will take money and time, but Bob has the faith and the energy.

"There are some really good things happening in my life right now, and it is all coming together," he says. "I really feel that I have a calling here. I'm not exactly sure where it is leading me, but I feel called upon to do something.

"Just the other day, I had a state hearing with one of my families, and when I shared with them my plan for developing this home for children, they were excited. They needed this house for their child yesterday. And I was telling them, 'Well, you know, it *is* going to take time and money.' But maybe that is my goal. I want to fight for them."

A CONVERSATION WITH BOB VOSS . . .

Homes seem to be a recurring theme in your life. A home is much more than four walls and a roof, but what does having their own home mean to people?

Part of it, I think, is a sense of achievement. If you build your own home or fix up your own home or whatever it is that you do to finally complete that dream of owning your own home, there's a sense that you've arrived at a certain level or place in life. It's a way by which you can measure your place in life. It's a yardstick. More important, I think, for me, a home gives a sense of identity, permanence, roots, family. This is where you grew up. This is who you are. I find that once mentally retarded clients have a place they can call their own, they are different.

How are they different?

Often, the mentally retarded live in group homes or facilities. These are not homes. They are licensed beds. The owner or provider gets paid to have someone sleeping in the bed. Often these are congregate settings with several people in one room, or certainly at least another roommate. These people never had their own place, their own room. They never had privacy, the dignity of having their own possessions. Their possessions consisted of whatever you could pack in a trunk and a closet, and a couple of suitcases. If the facility closed, they'd have to move somewhere else. It became kind of a nomadic life.

And that's what really hooked me with this whole supported living philosophy. It's not so much that they own the home. But rather, it's the control they have in that home. That's *their* home. They can dictate what they do, how their schedule works, who takes care of them. They have some control over their own destiny. They are making their decisions; I'm not making it for them. You are giving them an environment in which to grow.

When you talk about giving independence to the mentally retarded and allowing them to experience their dreams, you talk a lot about "the dignity of risk." Can you explain what that means?

When you are growing up, you learn to ride a bicycle. You start out and you've got somebody teaching you. Your training wheels are on. Eventually they are going to let go, take off the training wheels and you'll ride it by yourself. And you know there's a chance you are going to fall, and you'll scrape your knee and maybe chip a tooth, but you know what? That is the dignity of risk.

What I have tried to do, through the consent of parents and the consent of the clients, is to allow our clients to take some risks. It's their life. We're not here to live their lives, only to assist and tell them what's appropriate.

The dignity of risk isn't just a concept that applies to the mentally retarded, is it.

Everyone can apply that term to their life. It is hard as a parent. Your child grows up and wants to ride the bike, so you start with training wheels and eventually you have to take the training wheels off and you have to know, eventually, every kid who rides a bike crashes. It's not because they can't go up and down the street. It's when they get a lot better and they can go really fast, that is when they start to test the limits of their independence. It's something they have to learn.

I think that's what happens out of failure. It's not failure. Out of the pain and out of the defeat sometimes comes a lot of learning. Often that is what builds character. If everything is going great, well, that's great, but you can really learn a lot about a person when things aren't going well, from the kind of person who comes out of that, who rebounds.

But who makes the decision about how much risk a person can take? This was a big misperception in our field. It was the professionals, the parents, doctors, nurses. It is our job to protect. To make sure our clients are eating their 1,200-calorie a day diet. And guess what: When we started to ask the clients about this, they didn't like any of that. So maybe we have to teach them about making choices—about when to eat, what to eat, how much to eat. Maybe we need to teach them something, not just restrict them. Because when we are in control and we restrict, that's against their rights. Everybody has a right to fail, everybody has a right to take risks. As long as you inform them of what the consequences can be of taking those risks, good and bad, then they can make the decision for themselves.

In your work, you see so much that needs to be done, yet sometimes there is not enough financial or political support. How can we keep a dream alive in the face of disappointments and struggles?

I can only speak for myself. I've seen other people where they are defeated and give up. That's the hardest thing for me to see—when there is potential and you can't come back. You just don't have the energy to fight it any more.

I wouldn't say I portray myself as a religious person *per se*, but I have a belief in a higher power. Call it God or whatever you want to call it. I call upon that power at times when I'm alone at night, sitting there thinking about how I can't do it, how I can't control some things that are totally outside me. And I just say, "OK, I'm going to get up the next morning and whatever is going to happen will happen." Sometimes you just have to kind of let go and say if that's the way it is, that's the way it is. I'm not going to beat myself up over things I can't control. I share that with many of my clients. "Was this something that you could control? Was this something that was your fault? Was this something you brought upon yourself?" Sometimes you are carrying that baggage around and you are thinking it's your fault, it's your responsibility, you can't do it, you're a failure. And it worsens the situation, I think.

But how easy is it to let go and give up control? That's not human nature, is it?

No, it's not. I'm not saying you have to give in, that you have to stop fighting. I'm just saying that sometimes you have to let it go. Often you find that when you least expect things to happen, they happen. When you are trying your hardest to make it work, it doesn't. Sometimes you have to step away and say, "I'm not going to think about it today. I'm going to go do something for myself. I'm going to go play guitar." Just totally say "It doesn't matter what I do, so I'm just going to go do something for myself." Take care of yourself. Otherwise, you cannot take care of your business. So, be kind to yourself instead of taking the approach where you feel frustrated.

Our hopes and dreams often have to be adjusted to fit changes in our situation, don't they.

We all dream pie in the sky, and then we figure out where we are and we have to compromise. So our clients have to learn how to do that. They get the chance to test their independence and test some of their decisions. They experience the dignity of risk and they learn it's OK to fail. We all do. We all make mistakes.

You know, what we don't teach our mentally retarded clients is how to be more flexible and adaptive. As much as we try to make life stable and consistent, it's not like that. Sometimes you have to make a change and you have to learn to adjust.

When parents place their child in one of our programs, they think they are going to stay in one place forever. But they aren't. They stay there long enough that they have done everything they can do in this setting, and then it is time for them to move on. And there will be a transition period and they may not like it, but I guarantee you that after they get through it, they are going to look back and say, "Wow! I'm glad I did that because my life is so much better. I'll never go back to living there again."

Don't people sometimes crave consistency and constancy?

There's definite comfort in that. People want to wake up at the same time of day, have the same breakfast, go to work the same way, play the same tape. There is something valuable in that. If you can't predict something in life, it's not good.

But can't it be overdone?

I'm not saying it can be debilitating, but it does limit you. I find myself sometimes thinking, "Hey, wait a minute, why don't I do something different? Why are you going this way? Because I haven't ever gone this way." You never know what you might encounter, going a different way. I'm always up for that little surprise.

It seems you might be limiting your thinking and your dreaming if you aren't willing to go off the beaten path.

As I said, I was in the middle of the highway in a huge groove and that was fine. You can go really fast in the middle of the highway in the big groove, but you know what? You can't *see* everything. You can just see what's there from the highway. Sometimes you have to go off and venture around a little bit. I guess I'm feeling more comfortable with that.

Do we ever unintentionally put limits on the dreams of people around us?

I think often it is individuals who limit themselves rather than the circumstances. I know sometimes you can't overcome certain circumstances whether it is political, environmental or personal. If you feel as though there is a motivating force within yourself, I think you are better off than if you feel that outside factors control you. That can be even more limiting, when you don't feel you have the power to control or change your situation.

I'm more intrinsic. If it is something you really want, I believe it can come from within you—although sometimes there might be overwhelming external factors. I'm just saying that if you can persevere long enough, sometimes dogged persistence will crack through. I just feel that if most people put their mind to something, they can achieve some level of success and feel good about their accomplishments.

There are people who feel they have no control?

Oh yeah. They want no responsibility. You just want to shake them. You think, "OK, so what are you going to do? Sit there and wait for divine intervention? A lightning bolt?" It's kind of frustrating when people think they are just like a leaf blowing in the wind. Well, no, you're not. Sometimes people are just creatures of habit, going along their own way, thinking that must be the way I want to go and need to go because that's the way life has been. Well, you *can* change it.

Sometimes, those people do change. They dare to act on the dreams they have previously beaten down. What causes the transformation?

Often it is trauma. If life is relatively stable, you really don't have need for change. This is something that we see in counseling. Change comes about where there is discomfort. A good counselor doesn't want to make a client feel too comfortable because they aren't going to change. What you need to do is kind of strike a balance between making them feel a little uncomfortable so that they might want to change. So, discomfort is not bad, because sometimes that is the impetus for change.

Does trauma have to be the trigger?

It shouldn't have to be, but it often is. Something shakes you up and makes you question what you are doing. You do question when everything around you is out of control. But it is really nice when you have positive support, and your self-confidence is leading and you are taking risks because you aren't afraid to take a risk, because you feel it is OK. So it doesn't have to be trauma. It doesn't have to be a negative thing that forces you out of your comfort zone. It can be that things are going well. People are being positive and you are getting support and you are feeling like you know what you are doing, so why not climb the next plateau?

I feel that's what's happening to me. I feel like things are going well. I'm getting a lot of positive support. There is no reason not to venture out of the middle of the road—where it is kind of boring, actually. There are no hazards or anything.

Are you going to be prepared when you hit that bump?

Yeah, because I can reference it against some things that have happened before. I don't know how much worse it can get when you lose a parent or you have an act of nature impact you. Every day you see something on TV that reminds you to be thankful. Really, I don't complain. I don't like people who complain. And I don't like to be around people who complain.

The dreaming you do benefits others. What about your own dreams?

Some people wake up and say, "I'm going to be such and such" and they go and pursue that and get it done. I haven't had that clarity yet. I know I haven't had a clearly defined dream. Maybe I'm waiting for the divine calling. I just know I'm not done.

The neat thing about my parents is that they didn't push their dreams off on their kids, and so we were always allowed to have our own dreams. I see a lot of people pushing their kids in one direction and it doesn't become the kid's dream; it is the parents' dream. My parents never did that.

And I think you can change your dreams. Who said you only have one chance at a dream? I think that is the other misconception. "Oops, I'm sorry you were supposed to be a baseball player and now your dream is over. You are a failure. You missed your chance." Well, that's baloney. That sets up people for failure almost all the time. Very few people are going to be that one thing that everybody else thinks they should be. I think you can and should have some smaller dreams along the way. It doesn't have to be the grand dream where everything falls into place.

You've got some bigger dreams for your program, dreams that are going to cost a lot of money.

Yeah, and that's the catch. We've got some ideas on how to do that and how to fund it. In Lessons in Leadership's last book, there was one thing that caught my eye that Larry said, that you can have dreams, but you need a lot of people to help you fulfill them. You can't do it by yourself. And I realize that. I'm trying to get other people to help me with my dream. It's going to take a lot of collaborative effort.

Is that the key for any leader with a dream—to create a climate of collaboration?

It's one thing to have a dream, but is another to tell other people about it. I talk about it more than I used to. I realize that people won't know what it is that you are dreaming unless you share it. You have to get people behind you. I think that is how you start to build your climate for collaboration.

Everybody's got their own ideas of what they would like to do in their job. Maybe they don't have the same dream that I do. You've got to talk about your dream, then check to see where others are at. I'm finding out now that some people we recently hired are going to be real helpful in helping me do more things in my program. So there is that synergy, someone else catalyzing what I've got. And all of a sudden, we can do something that is totally new.

But I can't do it by myself. You need other people to fulfill your dream. You don't have the expertise. You've got to have a lot of people and abilities to attain a dream. And you have to be self-less sometimes in order to achieve a goal. And it may not be what you envisioned. That's the other thing. You have to be somewhat flexible. You can't just say, "No, this is the vision, this is the goal, this is what we are doing," because you might lose a couple of people along the way. You might have to massage it a little bit because everybody's got their own ideas.

What happens when others see dreams become reality?

I think it's contagious. If you can be motivated and upbeat, other people will feed on that energy. All of a sudden it goes from something they didn't even think about to something that is possible. When you dare to dream and it becomes a reality, it's a positive thing that catches fire. Our clients will talk to their friends and say, "I'm living in this house," and the friends will go visit and then they'll go home and start talking to their parents and say, "I'd like to live in a house," and all of a sudden it is like Pandora's Box. It is out there, and it's not me doing it anymore. It's them taking it and running with it. You can't squash it, you can't suppress it.

If you had to give advice to others about the importance of following dreams, what would you tell them?

For myself, it's never been about the tangible things. They *are* nice, great. You can show them off. You can touch them. For me, though, it has always been the intangible things when it comes to dreams. And that is where I think a lot of people mess up, because they think a dream has to be something you actually hold in your hand. Dreams can be personal relationships, spiritual growth, the things that make you stronger as a person. It's not so much about how many toys you have at the end of the day or how big your house is.

Do you think people sometimes believe that material wealth and dreams are synonymous?

We often link the fulfilling of dreams with money and the acquisition of some "thing." That's not what it is about for me. I think of my parents, and being up in our vacation house in North Carolina. We have the house and it is a physical thing, but what's important is the time you spend there with them— kicking back, playing pinochle or listening to Frank Sinatra.

Those are the things I remember. That is the kind of impact that I would like to have on people. Not that Bob Voss can buy houses and put the mentally retarded in them, and find providers and take care of them. I want to do it because of what they can do when they are in the house, and the happiness they feel.

Joanne Everett: Bell's palsy ended her career as an actress, but marked the beginning of a varied and productive life that now includes teaching in the Marshall Islands.

9

JOANNE EVERETT
ACTRESS, EXPLORER, TEACHER

"Try it. Nothing is forever.
If you don't like it, do something else."

I n our last book, we visited with Joanne Everett, a former
Southern belle from South Carolina who became a Chicago
actress, a talent agent and a mother of two. Joanne's experience of "neighborhood" was a little more far-ranging than
most. Not only did she make the transition in the 1950s
from the Deep South hamlet of Spartanburg, South Carolina, to the City of the Big Shoulders, but since the early
1990s she has lived and worked in the Marshall Islands, first
as a Peace Corps volunteer and now as a teacher.

In a life that has had its full share of setbacks, Joanne
nevertheless has moved from one dream to another, often
finding that, at the darkest moment, a new and fulfilling
adventure awaited.

"There has been a lot of synchronicity in my life," she
says. "I can't even begin to tell you about it. It's like the
hand of God is playing chess."

That's as good an explanation as any for her latest
manifestation. She's served as co-chair of the English Department at the College of the Marshall Islands. Now, at
age 65, she's returned to the islands to teach again.

151

The Marshalls are a nation composed of more than 1,100 tiny islands, "glorified sandbars anchored to coral reefs by stands of coconut and pandanus, surrounded by bright blue water," as Colin Woodard described them in a 1998 article for the *Bulletin of Atomic Scientists*. Ever since the atolls of the area were used by the U.S. government for nuclear weapons testing, the Marshallese have lived in a virtual welfare state, supported by compensation trust funds and Pell Grants.

When she first moved to the Pacific, Joanne lived on Airok, in the atoll of Ailinglaplap ("Big Island"). Today, she finds herself on the main island of Majuro atoll, where half the nation's population of 60,000 live. In Majuro's capital city of the same name, she instructs college students in English as a second language. The city is the cultural center of a nation gradually forging ties with the rest of the world, where young people of the current generation are setting a new standard for worldly knowledge and ambition.

It is an odd process, this sudden linkage with the global economy. As Woodard wrote: "The youth of the outer islands are drawn here (Majuro) by junk food, beer, electricity, high school and the hope of joining the cash economy." The world moves slowly in the Marshalls—"They are gentle, loving, kind people," Joanne says—but move it does. By helping some of them master English, she hopes to give them a foundation for dealing with the outer world that continues to exert more influence.

Joanne can relate to their clash of cultures. She remembers when she was preparing to leave her little hometown in South Carolina to study at Northwestern University's prestigious National Institute of Speech and Drama in Chicago.

"Nobody belonged to sororities where I came from," she says. "I got a notice on a postcard from Northwestern. 'I will rush' and 'I will not rush' were the choices. My mother and I didn't know what that meant. So we checked off 'I will rush,' and qualified it with 'I'll come by train.'"

After college, when many actors immediately pack their bags for the requisite trip to New York City, Joanne signed on instead with the Studebaker Repertory Company in Chicago, founded by Paul Sills, who would later found Second City—the improvisational comedy troupe that would become the training ground for emerging stars such as Dan Akroyd, John Belushi, Bill Murray, John Candy and a host of others.

"We would meet at Paul's place on LaSalle Street and do improv exercises all night," she says. "It was very small, and just great. I had never even heard the word 'improv.' They all had black clothing on, dressing like beatniks, and I'd be there in my little dresses. Paul said they needed me so people would think they were normal."

Under that prim costume, however, there blossomed an extraordinary person, a catalyst for so many dreams, so many connections. When Joanne entered this world, she was a breech birth in the middle of a thunderstorm. She gives nature due credit for her dynamic energy, but she alone has persevered in turning dreams into possibilities.

The Marshallese could have no better dream guide than Joanne Everett. Not only does she unceasingly chase down her own desires, but for a long time she has fostered them in others. From her early days as a local TV sock hop hostess in Richmond, Virginia, Joanne has had a knack for firing up people. She has played vital roles, on and off the stage, with theater companies in Chicago, as a Peace Corps volunteer and now as a far-flung leader in global education.

Sometimes she's had to fire up herself. After a divorce, she was thrust into the unexpected solo role of bringing up her two daughters. Then, in the early 1980s, she was struck with Bell's palsy, which left her with permanent nerve damage to her face. For many of us, that might have been difficult enough, but for an actress it had the potential to be devastating. However, her openness to change allowed her to transform her pain into further self-discovery.

"Bell's palsy was the biggest shock I ever had in my life," she says. "It changed my life overnight. It was worse than getting divorced. I couldn't work on camera anymore. So I went to work at a talent agency. I didn't know one thing about being an agent, but every day was a learning experience."

The woman who hired her was a dreamer in her own right.

"Her name was Emilia Lorence. She gave me a wonderful opportunity," Joanne says. "Everybody jumps on your bandwagon when you're winning, but nobody does when you're losing. She stuck with me. Emilia had struck out on her own herself, starting with very little money. She had a mental gift for talent. She could pick up people out of the woodwork."

It was not the first time that a door opened in the midst of personal setback. Much earlier in her life, in 1957, Joanne's mother was stricken with cancer. Joanne returned to Richmond, Virginia, to tend to her mom. Television was still a fairly new item, particularly local programming. "I saw an ad for a TV show in the newspaper," Joanne recalls, "and thought it was a joke."

But one day she was downtown shopping, and a woman in a store noticed Joanne and asked her if she was a model. No, Joanne said, she wasn't. The woman was adamant. Joanne should go the store's modeling department. So she did.

"And the lady there calls the TV station and says she's found the person to do the show," Joanne says.

She wound up hosting "Top 10 Dance Party," a local spin-off of Dick Clark's "American Bandstand." She interviewed teenagers and introduced songs. The program was sponsored by Coca Cola, and was aired out of one of the company's warehouses.

"I wound up doing that program for a year," Joanne says. "I had never been in front of a TV camera in my life. There were 18 people from Northwestern's Speech School graduating in 1956, maybe 10 of whom were actors. We had a radio school and they were just adding on TV, but we had no camera or studio. The concept was new, and how to perform on it was new. But life was simple then. It wasn't any big to-do. Now you have to have a Ph.D. and a million workshops, and then maybe you'll get an audition. But there were not so many people trying to get on TV then."

Joanne has that uncanny ability to cross paths with interesting individuals—and one in particular demonstrates just how small a world it is. If you're familiar with the idea of "six degrees of separation"—where it's said that any one of us is only six people separated from knowing anyone else in the world—you'll appreciate this story.

When we told her about Tori Murden, the trans-oceanic rower we discussed in an earlier chapter, she said she'd just had dinner the week before with a man rowing through Micronesia on his way to rowing around the world.

"He's just a plain old shoe," she says. "I didn't find out why he liked the risk so much, or why he had this incredible faith in technology. He thought it would not fail him. But I think the six degrees of separation is true. You will find out some way or another you are connected. You have more in common than you have differences."

Sometimes, the separation is less than a city block. From second grade through high school, Joanne was best friends with a boy named Fred Myers. The boy became a writer and now lives in New York City. "He was a Rhodes Scholar, and he's a true soul mate," Joanne says. "It's an inexplicable, mystical bond."

Before Joanne was sent to the Teachers of English to Speakers of Other Languages international conference in New York last year, she e-mailed her old friend. She mentioned that she'd be staying with her old Peace Corps buddies and maybe they should get together. She gave him the address.

Fred e-mailed right back.

"Oh," he wrote, "they live across the street from me."

Joanne beams at that one. "Talk about synchronicity!" she says. "We wound up going out every night to dinner together."

Fred, it turns out, was the catalyst to Joanne's acting dreams many years prior. In the third grade, the two decided to put on a play. And as they grew, their interest in theater remained. Fred wrote, drew cartoons in class, gave talks about T.S. Eliot ("Of course, the teacher had never heard of Eliot," Joanne laughs) and eventually would write operas.

"Fred introduced me to the theater, where for my first role I played a Cockney maid in a show called *Ladies in Retirement*," Joanne says. "That was how I made the acquaintance of another important person in my life, the school's drama director, C.E. Landrum. He was a great mentor for me during adolescence—a terrible, insecure time. All through my high school career he pointed the way to the "outside" world—yes, much the way I do for my students now. He's the one who got me into Northwestern's National Institute of Speech and Drama when I was 16. That experience alone was enough to let me know that taking a chance could have great rewards. Then I won a drama scholarship to return to Northwestern.

"C.E. supported and encouraged me without inflating me. I'd do battle with him to get a role, and he'd say I wasn't right for it. There was one play called *Eastward in Eden* where I wanted to play Emily Dickinson, and I hounded him. He gave it to somebody else. She couldn't do it because of something, and I ended up getting it. That was a breakthrough for me. It was like somebody else came and played that role. It was then I realized that this would be my field."

It's that intuitive ability that seems to fuel Joanne's eagerness for new pursuits when a roadblock gets in her way. Meanwhile, her profound belief in connection has been a long running current in her educational career, from teaching grade school as a newlywed in Norfolk, Virginia, to teaching English and literacy in Florida and now in the Pacific. Joanne, like the people who have nurtured her, passes on the favor to her students—and to everybody else, for that matter.

"I'm always running into interesting people," she says. "I'm aware of it, but not awed by it. Some people become deferential, but I just think those people are magic. Everybody puts their pants on the same way."

That's how Joanne sees the world—a world where it's OK to accept the extraordinary as almost commonplace, where delighting in other people—and the dreams they harbor—is an everyday occurrence. One of her favorite expressions is "What a hoot!" But she doesn't say it only when something's funny. She says it to all the interesting things going on around her. And she doesn't think it takes any special talent.

"I'm in no way exceptional," she says. "Adventuresome, but not exceptional."

Well, around the world—from Spartanburg to Chicago to Ailinglaplap—there are pockets of people who beg to differ. As with so many successful dreamers, it is those who strive to be open to such magic around them who often inadvertently wield that magic themselves. It manifests in their eyes, in their voices, in the ease and wonder with which they propel themselves through life.

Like the natural actress she is, Joanne Everett is also a natural born leader. You can tell because of the magnetic pull she exerts on people. Like so many others, we came back, too. We knew we had to talk with Joanne again.

"Your questions scare the living daylights out of me!" she said when we first approached her again. "I don't know if I'm introspective enough to answer any of them. I know the unexamined life is not worth living, but I've never been much of a navel gazer. I think I'm very boring, to tell you the truth."

We'll let you be the judge.

A CONVERSATION WITH JOANNE EVERETT . . .

How did you overcome having your dream shattered when Bell's palsy sidetracked your acting career?

Bell's palsy was the worst event of my life. How did I get the strength to dream a new dream? It wasn't easy and it wasn't quick. I have always had a strong faith. My parents gave me that gift—or maybe it is a gift from God. I know that when we have big trials in our life, it's for a reason—God's reason.

Then is when I listen very carefully to my inner spirit. And I also know that it is darkest before the dawn, that I'm being moved in a new direction. My job is to pay attention to the still, small voice and move ahead. That's when I became a talent agent. It was a good experience for me, and I think I brought good things to Emilia Lorence's agency. I'm a survivor, and I like to do it in style. I'm also very lucky to have good friends that supported me during the dark times. I was not alone.

Crucial moments in your life always seems to involve a strong connection with another person. Who are the people who have influenced you most?

Emilia was one of those people. No people have been bigger in my life than Bess and Sam Joyner. Bess and I have been best friends since we were in college together at Northwestern. We married each other off, birthed our babies, buried our parents. We have been witnesses to one another's life. I cannot imagine how I would have gotten through life without their support. Outside of my children, they are the most important people in my life. They are the family I have chosen, and they are as close as breath.

They have been an enormous gift to me. They have supported me and every event I have ever had in my life. Most recent example: When I decided on the spur of the moment to return to the Marshalls, without my asking they flew to Florida, helped me pack and close out my apartment and allowed me to ship things to their house where they are keeping them in storage while I'm overseas. When I questioned myself as to whether I was doing the right thing, Bess supported me and encouraged me to go. All my wealth is in my friends.

Have you always been so fearless when it comes to trying things you know nothing about?

My feeling after I went into the Peace Corps was, "Things that appear so difficult really aren't if you just do it." I'm a Nike girl! I now know that I could go anywhere in the world and survive. People are always there to help you. Most cultures are kinder than ours—or what we perceive ours to be.

Let's talk abut the Marshallese culture, for instance. It is incumbent upon them to take a stranger in—to feed them, house them and care for them. I pray that never changes, but it could.

They think nothing of it. I ended up this past Christmas on a strange island. A family I had never met took me in overnight without question, gave me dinner and the only mattress in their house to sleep on and got me to the plane in the morning. Some Marshallese person gave up his seat on the plane for me without my knowing it until I was in the air. That person had to wait another week before the plane returned and he could fly to Majuro. I don't know any American who would have done that! Island kindness is boundless, and I think it is because they are not hooked to time. There is no going back in our culture. Time is money.

What else can we learn from the Marshallese in conducting our daily lives and even our business?

The idea that family and friends come first—above all else. This is very hard for Americans or any other business people to deal with. If a Marshallese has a job and someone in their family needs them, they don't show up for work. They don't call in, and they don't understand why you get so bent out of shape. If your friend needs you, you go and help. Everything else can wait because it is not as important as your friend. Would that we could live like that, but our culture doesn't allow it. They still enjoy the humanness of life, and I hope it never disappears. Only time will tell.

Do you think the discipline of an actor enables decisive action in real life? Is there truth to the notion that if you act like you're doing something, before long you'll actually be doing it?

You learn to audition by doing it, by delivering where it counts. It was literally my living. Sometimes you don't even know why you say yes to something, but you do say yes. You just keep yourself open and don't try to figure it out. Think too much and you might not do something. Don't weigh the pros and cons all the time, just do it.

You have certainly said yes to the calling to go to the Marshalls. You've spoken before about the sheltered life led by the islanders. Have you ever felt that lifestyle resonating with your own Southern upbringing?

It's interesting on the islands. I feel very safe, very protected. I had never really connected that with my Southern upbringing, but it's true that I feel very loved and protected there, just like when I was a little girl.

Once a few years ago, I flew on the airplane with the American ambassador to the Marshalls. I was going back to the island of Irick for Christmas. They had their little color guard there waiting for the ambassador, with six policemen, three on a side, saluting. So I waited. There was such a huzzah. Then I walked out and there was an even bigger celebration. You'd have thought the ambassador was just an old shoe! Everybody on the island had come to meet me.

The family that I had lived with took me back to my old hut, which had been improved with some plywood. They had woven a gorgeous mat for me to sleep on. They had made seashell jewelry for me. I was wearing the same dress I had worn when I left. I immediately asked about the woman who had made it for me, and they said she was sewing dresses for people for Christmas.

So we went to the little church for Christmas. Each island in the atoll makes up a dance and song, and they perform for the other islands. Then they toss out candies for the children. They have a place of honor for the guests. So I sat with the American ambassador in the front. That afternoon, I told them, "I didn't want the place of honor, I want to sit with you guys."

What is changing about the Marshallese lifestyle, and what remains the same?

First, the Marshallese are perfect people in many ways. They don't make over you in a huge cloying way. You can go walking over to people's huts and visit. They let me move at my own pace, in my own little time, stopping in to everybody's house. They're wonderfully warm, happy to have you, and treat you like you just left yesterday. It's that familiarity.

The whole concept of dealing with just today is wonderful. You find something to eat and cook it. You wash your clothes and hang them to dry. It brings you back into contact with existence.

How is that simple way of life clashing with the growth of a city like Majuro?

In 1990, Majuro was still a shack town. Now there are department stores, the Outrigger Hotel, a movie theater, even Cubs games! People from all around the world are living there, mostly Asian and Australian. Now, it's an international welfare state, not just an American one.

People have caught on to the fact that as long as China looms as a threat, the Marshall Islands will be politically important. So everybody courts them, as they do most of the small islands there. We still use the atoll to test our missiles. We pop them over from California right into the lagoon. So now the Marshalls have discovered free money from around the world. The Australians have given us money for a computer language lab. I've gotten to be real friendly with the Australian embassy person. That will be the first grant I'll have written by myself. We'll establish a library, which can be a continuing project.

When I was first in the Corps, in training, I got the clue that many of the Marshallese weren't aware of being part of the bigger world. We had a cleanup day, with big bags. They were picking up blossoms and fronds and coconuts, and leaving the washed up plastic diapers. I said, "That's the garbage." They didn't know what that was. They don't know what to do with it. I don't know if it's an international problem or what. What will they do with that soft drink can? They throw it on the ground. I think we should clean it up, because the products came from us. But how do they get rid of the garbage? Landfill. It's killing the reef, and literally increasing the size of the island.

A recent news item reported that the Marshalls and some other island nations may lose their Pell Grant eligibility. How is this affecting your efforts?

We are locked in until 2004. But the college is expanding, and they seem to have faith that its growth will be supported. There is so much money being pumped into the country, so the college is trying to get the money put into a trust, so that it will be run by the interest. I hope that will happen.

The Marshallese don't have a strong concept of "the future." Bright people are the most troubled there. It was not uncommon in years past to have lots of suicides among them. I remember when a valedictorian hanged himself. It's not a large problem now, but it has been in the past. But now there are the beginnings of a future, of a world beyond the Marshalls. When you can see from one side to the other of the place you live, that's literally living on a dot of earth in the Pacific. They're very slowly catching on to the fact that education means a better job, even in their own country. They're just now connecting to the fact that maybe when they finish two years of community college, they could go to Fiji, South Pacific, or Hawaii. Before, only the landed gentry went to those places.

The grant for the computer language lab means it will grow from 10 to 20 computers. You should see the excitement! They can work on pronunciation, they can write, study grammar. Can you imagine coming in off an outer island and sitting down in front of a computer? They're making gigantic leaps. Now, hopefully, the concept of being bright and applying yourself, the American dream, is starting to infuse them. If we export anything, that's a good thing to export.

For those eager people, does continuous learning continually fuel new dreams? What are the dreams of this island culture?

I'm very close to my people there. The Marshallese give people like me respect and honor because I was Peace Corps, I speak their language, I know their customs. So I try to motivate them within the context of their own culture.

They all get The Speech. I start off with the question: "Why are we studying English?" Most of the time, I get the answer, "So we can talk to *dri balles* (white people who come with too many things). Or they say it's because they want to talk to Americans. I then ask them, "Ever seen a Filipino talking to a Thai?" "Well, yes." "They're speaking English," I say. They begin to see that it's the world language, the language of business.

These students will be the leaders of this country. If you reach one person in a whole year, that's something, because the country is so small that one person will make a noticeable difference. I teach developmental language and critical thinking. For them, that's handling a problem, which they're very creative with. Academic thinking is much more of a challenge for them—as it is for me.

In adult ed, everybody has fun. When you get to a university setting, everybody is trying to braintrust you. So I try to make most of my friends outside of academia, which is a little kingdom that does not really exist. And yet, I don't want to get out of it because I like my students too much. I sense a connection with them.

Last year, I conducted a program called "What's My Dream?" I asked them to write down what they dreamed of being. One little girl wanted to be a doctor. That blew me away. That's so alien for their culture. I can't tell you how far afield that is. And she didn't say "nurse," she said "doctor." I was so excited. One kid wants to be a senator. He's as bright as a new penny. I believe they can do these things. You have to believe in people. They pick up on it.

This is a very old culture, driven by a king and a caste system. The king has all the benefits by virtue of birth, and workers don't really have the ego to even imagine they can do better. We're motivating them, the working people, and it's a concept that's hard to get across. The lack of role models within their own culture is always a problem. Even people in government

... although it's a republic with elected officials, those officials are usually from that high class. From this same stage of development in the United States, we got leaders like Abe Lincoln. They're at that stage now. The world is possible for them.

How do you deal with the clash of cultures? How do you help preserve their dreams of solid community?

I try to fuel my students' dreams within their own culture. Show them the possibilities for them in Majuro. Learning to read opens the possibilities of books. Learning English allows them to read, enjoy movies, talk to English-speaking people, get a job where English is required, become a senator and represent their government around the world. It happens one step at a time. We can use computers almost as a magical toy. They slowly discover the possibilities for themselves, just the same as we do. Many have seen enough of *dri balle* culture that they do not want to leave their country. Can't blame their pride of that.

You seem to have become such a part of the local culture that you serve as one of those role models, as a model dreamer.

I'm not a great planner. I don't think you can figure it out. You just have to be open to life and unafraid. I've done so many things not knowing what the heck I was doing. The Corps asked me to teach English, I said no. They said, "I'll bet you could." And I did. You just have to try it. Nothing is forever. If you don't like it, do something else. It's hard to do that consistently, because you have to make a living. I'm afraid too, but you just have to get over that fear.

Have you ever kept a dream journal?

In Florida, I kept a little folder called "Dreams." If I saw something I wanted to do, I'd cut it out and put it into my folder. I loved a certain house, so I called the owner, whose card I'd put into my folder, and he'd just put an ad in the paper the day before. So you see, I think I have a guardian angel. I drove right over, talked to him, and rented the house on the spot. It was double the rent, but I found somebody to share it with me. I loved that little house.

So what's in that folder today?

I have the folder still, but I don't have anything in it. I would like to visit many of the Pacific cultures. I'd like to get to know the people and especially their art. There are so many things to do. Then I'd like to return to this country and travel to areas I've never been to. I'd like to come back from the Marshalls before I'm too old and get in a Winnebago and drive around.

What fuels this quest for adventure that you seem to thrive on?

What fuels my dreams of learning about other people and places? I don't know. I'm always afraid I'll miss something! Now that I'm 65, I realize that I cannot possibly live long enough to do all the things I'd like to do.

Harold Koning, therapist for individuals and a consultant for organizations, dreams of someday opening a healing center for those unable to afford professional help.

10

HAROLD KONING
HYPNOTHERAPIST, CONSULTANT, SYSTEMS BUSTER

*"You can design the quality of your life.
Just start walking. Start the journey."*

When Larry has a slew of marketing letters to write, he sometimes goes on retreat to a health spa to recharge his batteries and clear the decks so the marketing muse can inspire him. Such was the case in the late spring of 1997, when he went to Spa Atlantis in Pompano Beach, Florida, and chanced upon Harold Koning.

Harold was conducting a workshop centered on "dynamic wellness strategies." As it turned out, Harold was a walking, talking, kick-boxing bundle of wellness strategy himself—so feisty, funny and insightful that Larry went up to Harold afterward and signed him on the spot to conduct a workshop for WYNCOM employees.

Some things you should know about Harold:
- He moves like he's 20, talks like he's 30, looks like he's 40—and is actually 63.
- He speaks seven languages and has a doctorate in social psychology—even though he has attention deficit disorder (ADD).

- He is hyperactive—but once spent the first year of an intense Indonesian martial arts course doing nothing but standing still.
- He dreams—big time, all the time.

"I'm a systems buster," Harold says, tagging his observation, as he often does, with a chuckle. The systems he seeks to eliminate—be it an individual's or an organization's—are the ones that don't serve people well.

"People often come to me and they have a system in their mind. They've been programmed to view themselves in a way where they reduce themselves," Harold says. "What I do is to help them become a complete new system, because they start discovering their own capacities. You *can* design the quality of your life, if you so choose.

"Whether I'm working with an individual or a group or an organization, I always assume that there is knowledge there, there is wisdom there and there is experience there that has not been touched."

Which sounds like, to us, just the sort of attitude a good manager or leader should have as well.

Harold's latest vision is to establish along with his wife, Aurora, a healing center for people who can't normally afford therapeutic help. As a clinical hypnotherapist, business consultant and wellness workshop facilitator, he's dedicated to bringing out the potential in people. He regards people as clients, not patients. He goes into businesses not to offer "expert" advice, but to find, as he puts it, "their heartbeat"—so they can begin to genuinely change to become more efficient, creative and productive. When the system is healthy, dreams take flight. And in Harold's world, dreams are not to be deferred, but are instead guideposts to be honored and pursued.

What else would you expect from someone who, because of ADD, required nine years instead of the requisite five to get his Ph.D., who fled his native country of Surinam when several friends were murdered in a military crackdown, and who came to this country in 1982 as an illegal immigrant with only his family, four pieces of luggage and trepidation about what opportunity he would find here.

He's done quite well, thank you.

After a number of odd jobs including stints as a waiter, Harold was hired by the University of Miami in 1983 to train immigrants to bridge the gap between their cultures and American life. When grant money for the special program dried up in 1988, he spent 10 months selling educational programs for vocational training schools. The University of Miami re-hired him in 1989 to coordinate the revived immigrant program. In 1990 he became a school social worker for the Broward County School Board. Throughout, he was expanding his own private practice. Then, in 1997, he abruptly quit his job and set out on his own. A dream—establishing his therapeutic center—had beckoned.

For much of his life, Harold has had to overcome big obstacles to reach his dreams. Growing up in what was then known as Dutch Guyana, located on the northeast coast of South America, Harold showed such promise that he was offered a chance to study in Holland. He spent 1959 to 1963 there, receiving a master's degree in social work, and returned from 1972 to 1981 to pursue his doctorate in social psychology. Because of his ADD, it took three attempts to pass his dissertation. "Big deal," he laughs. "It took longer, but so what?"

It was that experience, in fact, that seared into his psyche the notion that labels can limit people and serve as obstructions to realizing their potential. Had Harold merely accepted the label of being an ADD "sufferer," he might never have attempted anything as daunting as a doctorate.

But the real challenge would come in his homeland.

Surinam had become an independent nation in 1954, shedding its old name of Dutch Guyana. It had a government that was, in Harold's words, "sloppy, but democratic." When Harold returned to Surinam from his studies in 1981, he was soon made a vice president of a national vocational training program. But a military takeover soon turned ugly.

"Cuba was trying to establish Communist regimes throughout the region," Harold says. "In December of 1982, the leadership in

Surinam killed 15 people at random. Four of them were very close friends of mine. And I found out that I was on the list, too."

So, on short notice, Harold decided to flee. He told people he was going on a trip to give a workshop in the United States, packed four bags, gathered his family and never looked back.

As he struggled to build a new career in a new land, Harold also went through a crisis of confidence. He believed firmly in the traditional models of therapy that regarded people as patients needing to be "cured." He established ongoing treatment with his clients, many of whom expressed their happiness in seeing him at session after session. Problem was, nobody ever seemed to get appreciably better. And Harold began to wonder if he wasn't depending on the positive feedback he was getting, rather than helping his clients improve.

"It was a painful process of looking at myself in the mirror, and looking at the jerk I'd been all those years professionally," he says. "I believed I was doing the right thing, because that's how I was trained. It was painful. I had some moments of doubt. I thought my career was going down the drain. I thought I'd have to go back to school and become an engineer. I even considered going and selling encyclopedias for a living.

"Now, in hindsight, I can say that it was basically that I didn't feel any sense of accomplishment."

Then, in 1990, he began to study the work of American pioneers like Milton Erikson and Albert Ellis, who helped introduced ideas of hypnosis and rational emotive therapy that Harold found intriguing. Moreover, all the training he'd done in the martial arts had heightened his awareness of Eastern thought. He'd gone, after all, from being a standard boxer to a kick boxer—his interest as keen in the philosophical and spiritual aspects of martial arts as it was in execution of the movements. He also went from being "Dr. Koning" to just plain Harold.

"I'm a success," he says, "when my clients say, 'Harold, I don't need you anymore. I can do it myself. I practiced this thing, and it works.'"

So it has, with numerous people and organizations. Harold once worked with a prominent attorney who owned a large law firm. The man was not happy in his work, felt many in his firm of

45 people detested him, and felt the same about many of them. Every two years, the man bought himself a new Rolls Royce. "So I put him on a fast," Harold says. "A Rolls Royce 'fast.'"

The result?

"He was yelling and screaming," Harold says with a laugh. "He tried to bargain out of it. He asked if it might be OK if his wife drove him to work in the Rolls. I said, 'No, you rent a Chevy Lumina and you go to work with the same attitude you've always had when you hand your keys to the valet.'"

"Harold," the man said, "this is going to *kill* me."

"Well," Harold replied, "let me know when the funeral is."

It worked. It's hard to be haughty, after all, when you're giving a valet the keys to a Lumina. After his initial embarrassment and awkwardness, the man seemed to lighten up, and so did the people around him.

"His attitude was linked to the Rolls," Harold says. "His status, his prestige, his impressiveness. He'd confused identity with image, and was always having to defend that image. He always felt he had to be on top of everything and everybody."

Meanwhile, Harold no longer finds himself estranged from his homeland. Democratic elections returned to Surinam in 1989, and Harold discovered he was no longer in danger. In 1992 he went back for the first time since his escape, and he visits there regularly now, occasionally conducting workshops. Living just outside Fort Lauderdale in Plantation, Florida, he continues to see individual clients, hold workshops and consult with organizations—all the while building toward the dream of having a healing center someday.

He also can still launch a rather awesome above-the-head kick.

In the blink of an eye.

A CONVERSATION WITH HAROLD KONING . . .

Your work in some respects is all about dreams—allowing people to dream, to have hopes, aspirations, goals.

Yes. It's all about improving the quality of life. And it goes to dreams. Sometimes it goes to lucid dreams, sometimes it goes to hypnosis, sometimes it goes to imagery and visualization. That's how people dream and go on to self-realization.

Dreaming is, in one sense, a metaphor for having goals and vision, but in your work, dreams—actual dreams—can be significant.

Dreams are part of the subconscious mind, the inner self, or the higher self. When a person dreams, the subconscious mind is expressing what has been suppressed during the day because of all the rules and the regulations and the "musts" and the "shoulds."

So when people really restrain themselves during the day, they stop the functioning of a very important part of themselves which some people refer to as intuition. I call it your soul intelligence, or your heart intelligence. That's the subconscious mind in a nutshell. It's a spontaneous element that does not analyze, does not discern . . . it just goes, if you give it the opportunity.

So how important is it to pay attention to those dreams?

Very important, especially when you have recurrent dreams. If a certain theme is coming back on a regular basis, you have to stop and think about it. But most people don't know how to do that, they don't know how to go "inside," because most people don't meditate.

What can the dream be?

A dream can be a message. It can be information. It can be a need that a person has been suppressing for a long, long, long time. And that's how our subconscious mind expresses itself, among other things.

So if you pay attention to that, you can realize dreams in the waking world—because it can make you clear on what really matters to you?

Yes, exactly. What I encourage people to do, once you have a dream that has a recurrent theme, sit down, be quiet, switch off your phone, put the dog outside, don't have any access to the external world, and *think* about that dream. And think wildly. Free associate. Any idea that comes up, just jot it down, write it down, without judging. Work with that dream. Play with it. Fantasize on it. And surprisingly, people come up with bright ideas of changing lives, of changing careers, of doing things for themselves healthwise. A lot of things come through. But people need to sit and make the time. The quiet time is very important.

What I do, I teach people what I'm practicing myself. I teach them a basic, simple meditation where they can be quiet—and then the information comes. You sit and pick up things because you've got all kinds of images and sounds and colors—and people can do it themselves, before they go to an "expert."

Is that one of the biggest problems in this culture, where everything is fast, fast, fast and we've got so much information coming in that we never take the time to reflect?

Oh yes, of course. This culture does not allow for quiet time. And people don't realize how they've been conditioned to be in a constant rush. It's "more, bigger, faster."

What's lost in that environment?

You lose what I call your natural intelligence, your soul intelligence, your heart intelligence, your physical intelligence. Most people don't even listen to their bodies anymore. When the body starts expressing some pain or ache, they go and have a quick fix. Numb it, so they can go on with what they're doing. So the "doing" has become the central part and people have stopped living as a human *being*.

Can anyone lead effectively when they're that out of touch with themselves?

No. What they're doing is, they're bossing around, and they're following fixed patterns. I work with many corporate leaders, and they have a fixed pattern. This is what they do, this is their goal, this is the deadline . . . and they never think out of the box. That's why they can't be creative.

And those who are creative and do things that nobody else can, like the Silicon Valley people . . . they do things that nobody else does, businesswise. And you see what the results are. They let the natural, raw, instinctive, intuitive creativity break loose, and you see what's happening. And that's the same thing I'm doing in my work with people.

What do you think would be an effective approach for a leader who is caught up in fixed thinking and doesn't reflect enough to break out of the pattern?

Take quiet time on a day-to-day basis, and listen for what's behind the words of others—and your own words. Taking quiet time is an effort for most people. The other day I did a workshop with 12 top people in one of the large telephone companies here, and I was practicing just this with them. They were talking about stress, how you walk into a meeting, you're stressed, you're tight. So I told them that, before you start the meeting, let me show you how to make the best of it. During the exercise, some of these people opened their eyes and said "It's hard! It's too slow!" I said, "Well, when you slow down, you can always pick up speed again. But you have to know you have the option of slowing down and recovering."

People don't take recovery time. So what is happening is that they are running from one unfinished business to another and they carry with them an emotional burden of "Oh, I still have to attend to that!" and they have a calendar full of things, so they just can't pay attention. They aren't there. Do you see people who go to meetings with a stack of paper with them, and while the meeting's going on, they are leafing through their own papers? They're not even there.

People confuse a flurry of activity for actual progress?

Yes. And on the other hand, part of the subconscious program that people have is, "Look busy and you'll look important." And everybody's impressed.

It's easy to get trapped into that kind of thinking. People might have an impressive to-do list and lots of "goals," but perhaps they don't really have dreams.

That's right. They don't have a "to be" list. That's why I make a distinction between "human doings" and human beings. We meet a lot of people who are human doings. And they just don't take time to work on the human being part of themselves, so they don't grow—or they grow in a certain direction and they think that's all there is.

Is part of the problem perhaps that, in the business community generally, tangible, immediate results are stressed so much that people can't see the value in more reflection? There's not a bottom line immediately?

No, there's no bottom line and there's never an end to it. Especially with the deadlines and the production requirements. People have to produce so much. I worked with a stockbroker, and they're driving him crazy. The guy made $40 million for his company last year. Now they're saying "Why don't you push it to $50 million before we get to the year 2000?" It's never good enough!

How do you combat that?

By saying no! "I'm not going beyond that, and I'm *not* going to put in 17 hours a day!" But most people can't say no. They're afraid of losing their job, there's a fear of rejection, a fear of looking stupid or not being professional . . . so there's a whole set of fears that have been programmed into people so they don't take care of themselves, because they don't know how anymore.

What would be the antidote?

The antidote is just to say "No, I'm stopping here," like I did. And many people I work with now are saying, "OK, this is where the work stops. This is how far I go."

And damn the consequences?

The consequences can be many, but you know, people have options to deal with the consequences. You can almost calculate your consequences.

How so?

For instance, I made the decision in 1997—in February, the third Friday—I told the people I worked for at the school board, "Next Monday, I won't be back. I'm not working for you anymore." Solid job, well paid, benefits, the whole nine yards . . . four years away from being vested.

One consequence? I don't have a pension plan. Do I care? No.

Another consequence: That Friday evening and that Saturday and Sunday I worked my butt off to make all kinds of calls, and the first week I made more money than I'd made in a whole month. That was one of the consequences. So when people say "consequences," they almost always think of something negative, but they don't have to be negative.

People give up that ability to affect their consequences, then. Instead, they think they're safe by following the status quo.

Yes, because people have been programmed to believe that that is the only thing they can rely on. I ask many people I work with in corporations what's going on. I do what I call a climate study; I want to know what's the atmosphere, what's the emotional situation here? And one of the things I discover is a lot of fear. People tell me "You can't speak freely here." I ask, "Why can't you speak freely?" They say, "I don't know how people are going to take it, and I'm not going to risk my job." These are people who have worked at places for 10, 15 years.

Now, where's that fear coming from? It must be part of the whole situation. And these are people who are well educated, well trained, who have a lot to say and have excess skills.

You're an independent spirit. Have you always been able to dream and not confine yourself?

Yes. Definitely so. And that has caused me a lot of trouble. Some people are just naturally dreamers. We have that special faculty.

What's the price of being that way and what's the reward?

The reward is that you live a healthy lifestyle and you become independent from other people's shoulds and musts, and the rules and regulations. You become very independent in terms of not being susceptible to the pressures that often force other people to do things. For instance, like living in a certain neighborhood, having to have a certain expensive car, or having to shop at certain places. All these things I don't have to have. I can pick and choose.

But you have to be willing to accept the fact that some people are not going to like you. So I know that many people don't like me, but what I'm discovering now is that there are more people who respect me, because very often they say, "I wish I could be as crazy as you." And I tell them, "Just start today."

The other side of that coin, it seems, is that with the people who *do* like you, you know it's more genuine.

Yes. It's pure, it's raw, it's natural. No doubt about that. So what you're seeing in the process when you make your own decisions and you go away from conventionality . . . first they call you controversial, then they call you arrogant, then they call you stupid, all these labels for you. As long as you know who you are and where you're going, all these labels are going to be just that, people's opinions. They don't know your truth.

Now the key question to get to that level—with what I'm teaching people, and what I've experienced myself—is every day you need to ask yourself, "Who am I?" In relationship to money, in relationship to prestige, in relationship to status, in relationship to fill in the blank.

And the second question I ask myself every day is, "Is my health my highest priority today?" Then I answer this with a yes, so I automatically choose and select three things I'm going to do that day that contribute uniquely to my health.

Is there a way to reconcile operating in a system and still being true to yourself?

Yes. My own experience, I still operate within a system, but I don't compromise myself. I don't sell my soul. You have to realize, we all have dreams. I hear people's dreams all the time. They speak about them, but somewhere there is a barrier of fear—a mental and emotional barrier of fear. They might have fear of losing their fiancé, their children, their job, of looking stupid . . . a lot of fears have been instilled because society is ruthless in punishing you if you step off the line. So, I work to get people out of this vagueness (of fear). But to break through is not that difficult. It's just that most of the time people don't know who they are, they don't know what they carry with them, and that's where they're stuck.

So how do you develop that ability to dream and be true to yourself, but not become at war with a system that isn't set up to reward that kind of behavior?

Well, the system generally is going to try to be at war with you, because those people who represent the system want you to stay in place. But you just do it. You're not going to be able to avoid war at times. It's part of being different. It's part of being unique. And uniqueness is not rewarded.

Part of being a good leader as well?

Oh, yes—if you're a real leader and not a boss. Some people are leaders, and some people are bosses. Now, the boss is going by power. The leader makes sure that he or she activates the leadership qualities within the group, and the leader has a philosophy that says leadership is a group activity. For instance,

"I'm in this official position. Let me see what else my people around me know, so I can put it together, consolidate it, and we have a program of progress." Then we have a team. But the rest is just bossing around.

Most people are running things that way because there's no trust between people who call themselves leaders and the rest of the people—and vice versa. So, trusting yourself and being aware of the fact that changes are going to take place and some people are not going to like it is essential.

You have to reflect, "To whom do I have to go and justify and explain what I'm doing, and why?" If people ask me, I give them an honest answer. This morning I got a call, "Can I see you this afternoon?" and I said no. "Why?" "Well, I'm booked until 4 o'clock and after 4, I don't work today." "Yes, but I really want to see you, Harold." "I understand that. Let me look at my calendar, and see when I can fill you in." I hold my ground. How many people do that? Letting go of an appointment at $125 an hour? How many have that financial freedom? I mean, I'm not filthy rich, but I've made a decision for myself today. My health is my highest priority today. And today at 4 o'clock I'm working out.

Do you see more businesses starting to recognize the importance of the uniqueness of the individual?

Yes, I do see them recognizing it, but most aren't acting on it. Most of it is lip service.

Why the discrepancy between talking it and walking it?

Fear. Fear of change, fear of rejection, fear of "It won't work." Fear of the unknown. I try to tell people who've had initial success with their organization but are reluctant to change from outmoded systems, "Look, all of the things you have started, you had no clue. It was the unknown. You stepped into the situation, took a risk and now it's working. So what's the problem here?" And when they say "fear of the unknown," I tell them to step into it and get to know it, then. But there's a reluctance there, and a lack of trust in people.

So the answer is, you just go ahead and attempt it, recognizing that you're not going to have positive change if you don't.

Yes, and if you can't do it on your own, we can coach you.

Which is a big difference—to help a company not as an "expert" consultant, but more as a coach.

Yes. Too many consultants don't come in as a coach, but as an expert. And they restructure communications systems, and it's mostly technical and financial. It's mostly thinking inside the box. So I go in saying, "OK, start trusting your people and find out what their special skills are. Make them your partners." That's difficult for most leaders. That's because they have to give away information, and that's part of their power game.

Difficult, but essential, if you really want to improve your organization.

Yes. Those who really want to make an organization for the new millennium must start building on their success. I believe leadership is a group function. I might have the official position of CEO, but I don't have all the knowledge, nor the experience of making the place run. So I need to depend on the people I hire, and I need to start trusting them.

And the notion of who's the leader fluctuates. Given the particular need at the time, someone might step up to be the leader of the moment.

Yes. It can be within a meeting or for a week or for a certain program, it doesn't matter. But the question is, are organizations willing to create the conditions—financial, social, physical and emotional—to allow that quality to come to the fore?

Once you cultivate the ability to know what you're really about and to dream big, can your dream become more

expansive and bring others in, allowing them to reach their potential?

Oh, definitely. Especially when you do it on a day-to-day basis. And that's the key, because we all have wonderful dreams. One of my dreams, I want to have that comprehensive healing center to gather with other people. I'm working toward it. That is something that is going to happen someday. Now, in the meantime, every day I'm doing things that are contributing to it. I'm being led and guided by that dream because it's really clear in my mind. I can see the building, I can see the premises, the whole nine yards. But I'm very realistic. I'm working every day one day at a time.

And I'm getting people's attention by example, among other things. People start asking me questions, it's sort of like radiation. You radiate something like freedom or calmness, and others begin to feel that as well. But living the dream means being practical and functional on a day-to-day basis within the reality of society, and people in society have limitations. So I don't expect everybody to immediately understand what I want or am pursuing.

And the other thing I do, when people ask me a question, I never volunteer advice unless it's asked for. I give them all the knowledge I have and I refer them to other resources, but I'm not running around on a mission. And that's what several people get into trouble with, because they want to convince everybody that this is the way to do it. I know what's best for me, and I'll show people the results of what works for me and then I'll tell them, "Find your own way. I'll show you varieties. I'll help you to find resources." But most of the time, living by example and teaching by example is really the best way to have others share in your dream, or begin to pursue their own dreams.

Why do you think people look to external validation for their pursuit of dreams?

Because people have been raised like that. And, of course, all human beings have a sense of belonging. We want to belong to something, or some place. That's normal, natural. All societies have a system, of course, where they socialize people. They teach you how to behave so that you don't mess up the place. But what I'm discovering is that, especially in this society, too many people are looking for approval by others—based on certain standards of dressing or walking or working or socializing. Too many people look for acceptance from the outside. "Accept me because I'm beautiful. Look at my breasts, look at my dress, look at the other nine yards . . . look at my car." And too many people are looking for love and being liked from the outside.

The other thing is the system of instant gratification. People want to have things *now*. That's why this society is so full of credit cards and sick people. Those three things—approval, acceptance and being liked—run very deep. That's why I tell people that, every day, you have to ask yourself "Who am I?" Start approving yourself. Start self-acceptance and self-love. And you don't have to be selfish to do that. You can be very realistic. I love myself, I practice every day, and out of that come my own values and dreams.

Success to me is, I've worked 30 hours a week—that's what I'm going to do—and the other hours I'm going to spend quality time for myself and with my family. That's my formula for success. I can work 50 or 60 hours a week making money if I choose. The option is there, but I set my own limitations. The other thing I'm not doing, I'm not putting myself into all kinds of unnecessary debts because I "have to" have this.

One of the things Aurora and I did in terms of our own "downsizing," we moved from semi-suburban Sunrise, Florida, to the house we have now. We don't have the pool. So what? We don't have the microwave. So what? We don't have the dishwasher. So what?

Personal downsizing has led to more expansive living, it sounds like.

It leads to freedom. It leads to happiness. You need to know that you have your basics already, and everything else is a perk.

Now and then we really go crazy and we go to 15th Street Fisheries and we eat for $90 an evening. Wonderful, great food! But I don't want to do that every day.

When you first came to the United States, it was hardly under ideal circumstances.

No, I was an illegal immigrant.

Were you in a survival mode, or were you able to dream even then?

Well, I was in survival mode *and* the dream was there, because I left a society and a culture that I knew—Holland and my country, Surinam—and came to a society I didn't know. Or I knew just partly. So that, among other things, gave me the opportunity to look at myself in a completely different way and identify for myself, thanks to the help of other people, what my special skills are. What makes me be me? What are my special qualities that I could put to work here?

You were not only entering a culture you didn't know well, but also one you didn't trust at first, right?

No, I didn't trust it and didn't like it. I was very prejudiced. Highly prejudiced. And I must say, up to today, several of my prejudices are still coming out. I don't want to be a number, I don't want to fit in, I don't know how to fit in.

Yet in many respects most everybody feels that way to some extent. There's a feeling of being disconnected from themselves, their dreams and each other.

Yes. People dare not be themselves. But what I discovered is that I could do things that other people didn't want to do, or didn't care to do because they thought there was no money in it. So when I made my resume, all kinds of things came to mind and I'd put them down—things you might not normally include— and so now my resume looks different than others. "I'm highly intuitive." It's in my resume. Not that I'm sending out resumes, but there's a metaphysical element in mine. If I would have to look for a job now, that resume would go out just like that.

So I've had the opportunity of looking at myself in a different way, and a very constructive way—with the help of others. In the past ten years, I've had a much more in-depth look at myself. And every day, really, that's the key, asking myself, "Who am I?"

For instance, last night in my meditation I was relating to this conversation we were going to have. So, "Who am I when you call?" And I meditated, and decided to just go with the flow, because it's a matter of absolute trust with you. That's what the meditation showed me. Absolute trust. Go open. Just see what happens. Just go with the flow. But with somebody else I'm going to meet later in the day, I have a completely different approach. Meditating gave me completely different information.

So I relate to each person differently, because I respect and I'm affected by the uniqueness of every person I'm meeting with. That's why I cannot see fifteen people a day in my practice. If I have four clients a day, that's it. That's how far I can stretch myself. And also, to be truthful to my own philosophy, I respect the people I'm working with, so I need to be there for them fully. I'm a "being" right there. And being is a very dynamic way of living.

Businesspeople talk about vision statements. To have a genuine vision and one you can lead others to buy into, how important is it that it be based on a genuine dream of what you want to accomplish, as opposed to just reaching a certain bottom line?

It's believing in people. That's the general state of affairs. Believe in people and the goodness of people. If you've read Anne Frank, at the end of her book that's what she says—basically all people are good at heart. I go by that. I literally go by that. And sometimes people have taken advantage of me. So what? That's part of the game.

So the general dream is there, and you work toward it on a day-to-day basis. Anne Frank and other people, that's what is positive. I always look at people's potential. I don't go by what other people say, like "Watch out for him, he's a bully!" or "Watch out for him, he's a shark!" That's their perception. I go and I find that other element, that potential that the other person isn't seeing—because I have the freedom. I can meet them without any preconceived idea.

It's one reason I call the people I work with clients and not patients. I'm looking for their potential as human beings. And it comes out if you give people the opportunity to be themselves. Most people are afraid to be judged, and they're judging themselves based on external standards. If you let them be who they really are by not judging, you can help them awaken their potential.

And people who reach their potential have to be able to dream?

Well, people *are* dreaming. The only thing is, they don't listen to their dreams. They listen to other people. A guy I worked with a few years ago, he listened to everything his parents said. Because they came from a long line of lawyers, he became a lawyer. Then he became an alcoholic, because his dream was history and French literature. He'd been told if he didn't become a lawyer, he would not be part of the will anymore. So he complied, because of greed and money and material things. It was driving him crazy. He came to the conclusion he had to break loose from this. The man went deep inside and his soul started speaking. He discovered all the pain he had. He discovered he was lying to his soul, and he was living an image. Well, you know how many people live an image and aren't themselves. They don't know their identity.

Have you noticed more receptivity from people to try new approaches because they realize there's something missing?

Depending on the source. If the source is reliable and the source looks genuine. For instance, when I stand in front of a group of people, I can honestly tell them what I'm telling you here. They can see it's genuine. And people are willing to listen. They come to the conclusion that there is another way. You can still be spiritual, but you don't necessarily have to be religious. And you can still make a lot of money—if you want to. But do things for yourself. Do things that you like, that you love, that are good for you. It's not an automatic, natural need out there, that people want to know (what's missing). But once they meet a person who appeals to them, then some people start asking questions and want to make changes in their lifestyle.

My philosophy is, when I do a presentation I count on 5 percent of the people paying attention. The remaining 95 percent are going to ask questions like "Yes, but . . ." and "What if . . ." and "Isn't this stupid, isn't this dangerous?" These are the majority of questions I get. But 5 percent are going to be genuinely interested because they've been on that quest already, but they didn't know where to go. A lot of them have burned their fingers by meeting all kinds of people you meet in the Yellow Pages—tarot readers and palm readers and what have you.

Most people have a sensitivity where they know whether you're genuine or not. When you're genuine and honest and warm and close and a real human being, people really relate. Those who want to make changes look for that. They're waiting in the wings to find somebody who inspires them.

Is that the trait of all great leaders, that genuineness?

Yes. Genuine, pure and honest. And also being able to admit that you're a little stupid and foolish and made a mistake. "Hey, listen, I goofed here. I made a stupid mistake. How can you help me?" Sometimes I walk into an elevator and I say "Today I'm going to feel *extremely* dependent on somebody!" People think I'm absolutely independent, but that's not true. I have my limitations.

If people are indeed waiting in the wings for inspiration, does that imply another key element of a leader—the

ability to create a climate that allows others to pursue their dreams?

Yes, that's the key. Create a climate. Make them a partner in whatever you're doing and become their partner. Most people will know that you are with them, not against them, not *over* them. That's why I make a distinction between boss-ship and leadership. Leaders are *with* their people. They trust their people. They are warm. They are there, and they also show their own weaknesses. Otherwise you don't have people working for you. The key thing is, be with people who can feel, "Hey, this guy is with me." And some people are going to take advantage of you, but again, so what? You can't get a hundred percent.

It seems that's a real problem. A lot of leaders believe that some people are going to take advantage, and they use that as justification to be oppressive and stifle everybody.

That's so right. And that is based on a basic insecurity of the person. When I have somebody who is working with me or for me—however you want to say it—and that person is much better than I am in a certain area, oh boy, I am going to use them because I love to work smart, not hard. Let that person excel! So I'm going to push it forward, "This is what John does, this is what Ellie does." And I'm going to show what every person accomplished. "*Look* at this person!" And it's easy to be that way. I have no fear of looking stupid or not in control. If I don't know how to do something, I just don't know how to do it. Period.

It sounds as if you're saying that, in leading people, you can expect to have bumps in the road, but don't let that make you forget that the pavement is still headed in the right direction, and you'll get there.

Exactly. And the other thing is, take your time. Like the Chinese say, the destination is there. Just start walking. Start the journey.

Juliet Mee: In the face of disillusionment, her resolve stiffened to awaken her community to the benefits of massage, alternative medicine and complementary medicine.

11

JULIET MEE
BUSINESS OWNER,
REBEL WITH A CAUSE

"Deep within the dream is your highest potential."

Often, being a dreamer is not easy, not a path the faint-hearted should pursue. There can be battlefronts facing dreamers at every turn, challenges on every corner.

And enemies. We all know them, those well-entrenched foes that have been waging war since the first dreamer stepped off the beaten path and onto a road of his or her own making.

Tradition, prejudice and the fear of anything new or different. Sound familiar?

Juliet Mee knows those enemies up close and personal. Over the years, at virtually every step along the way, she's had to battle them—becoming, in effect, a rebel of sorts, not by design, but by circumstance. It's been anything but easy. And when you add age and gender to the list of prejudices hurled her way, it becomes even more clear just how great a challenge Juliet has faced.

And overcome.

"I didn't consciously set out to make things so difficult for me," Juliet says. "I just wanted to do something

189

that counted, that was positive. To work with people and to help them in some way. That's really all I wanted out of life. How was I to know that the road I took was going to bring on all this controversy and all these struggles? I didn't know, that's for sure."

What Juliet did, while just barely past her twentieth birthday, was to start her own business, Natural Touches, in her hometown of Springfield, Missouri. There was just one problem. Her business—massage therapy—had a dreadful reputation.

"Back then, when you said 'massage' it was generally assumed that what you really were talking about was prostitution," Juliet says with a chuckle. "Of all the early obstacles I had to overcome, the prostitution stigma was the toughest. It was especially hard for me, being a 20-year-old female in a small Midwestern town. I used to hear comments like 'I would never allow my husband to get a massage.' It was tough. And being so young, I didn't have the know-how or the confidence to take on other people's belief systems."

Juliet, 34, can laugh about it now, but at the time it was anything but humorous. She was discouraged, threatened and distanced by city officials. Despite the wall that stood in her way, Juliet wasn't deterred. Armed only with a dream and a burning desire to make something of herself, she set about silencing her critics in the only way she knew how—by letting her performance speak for itself.

In a way, you could say she let her fingers do the talking.

"I apprenticed with a friend of mine named Melba Smith for about three years," Juliet says. "She was an excellent teacher. I learned everything from her. Her influence on me was enormous.

"With the background and training Melba provided, I became very, very good at what I was doing. There were very few massage therapists at the time, which was also a big plus for me. But the more I did it, the more my reputation grew. I became more and more popular. Word-of-mouth advertising was my big savior."

At the time, Juliet was making ends meet by working in a restaurant and in a card and gift shop. When she got off work, she would load her portable massage table into her old VW and drive to people's homes to give late-night massages. She did in-home massages for 10 years, and it was during this period, thanks to her growing reputation, that she made the decision to become completely self-employed.

"The truth is, I never really thought about being self-employed," Juliet admits. "I just never could get hired with the skills I had. Also, it didn't help that I am so fiercely outspoken. I say what I think, which isn't always a good thing. Now I can see that it was just my entrepreneurial spirit. When people see an entrepreneur, the last thing they want is to hear what's on their mind. Entrepreneurs are usually an employer's worst nightmare. I suppose that's because you need a rebel spirit to be an entrepreneur, and employers don't particularly care for rebels."

And so, out of the back of her Volkswagen, Natural Touches was born. The business, which began as a one-woman show, proved so successful that Juliet now has seven therapists working for her.

Juliet says she's not sure where her entrepreneurial spirit came from. She was born and raised in Springfield, the second of four children. Her father was an attorney, her mother is the director of the Management Development Institute at Southwest Missouri State University. It was from them, Juliet says, that she learned compassion.

"I've always enjoyed people and wanted to help them," she says. "I like being around them, to help ease their troubles. I think that comes from my parents. They were great. They taught us to love, respect and help people. *All* people. My parents were not prejudiced in any way. I grew up around all kinds of people."

Although there was nothing in her background to indicate a budding entrepreneur, Juliet says that spirit has been with her from the beginning.

"I've always been an entrepreneur," she says. "When I was a kid, I thought of a million ways to make a buck. I mowed yards, walked dogs, baby-sat. Anything I could do to make money, I did. It was interesting to me, doing so many different things."

Like most young people, Juliet assumed she would be college bound after completing high school. However, after graduating from prep school, she soon learned that the money for her college tuition hadn't been set aside. Undeterred, Juliet decided to teach herself something that was totally new and alien to her—alternative medicine.

It was this decision, the most crucial of her life, that led to her success as an entrepreneur.

Juliet needed a mentor, which she found in Dr. Norm Shealy. Dr. Shealy was the head of an alternative medicine clinic, where Juliet quickly volunteered to work, and the inventor of Tens Unit, a non-invasive pain management technique that was once highly controversial but is now widely accepted within the traditional medical community.

"I have absolutely no idea why I was so interested in alternative medicine," Juliet says. "Maybe I was just enthralled with Dr. Shealy. I met him when he moved to Springfield. Then I heard him speak when he came to visit our health class. He was fascinating and interesting to listen to. And what he said made complete sense to me. I was intrigued by alternative medicine, and its application, from the beginning."

So, although not yet out of her teens, Juliet had two consuming passions—massage therapy and alternative medicine. It's hard to imagine any young person choosing two more difficult or precarious career choices. Or two held in such low esteem by the general populace. One was linked to prostitution, the other linked to quackery and fraud. It's not exactly what your high school career counselor would recommend.

But as Natural Touches' reputation continued to grow, and the prejudices against massage therapy slowly began to crumble and its benefits began to be heralded, Juliet started to seriously explore ways to turn her dream of more involvement in alternative medicine into reality. Once again, though, she was met by overwhelming skepticism and nonbelievers.

"It's just not easy going against traditional beliefs," she says. "That's especially true when it comes to medicine and health. We've been conditioned to believe that there is only one way that works—the old, traditional way. It's hard—and in many cases, impossible—to get people to change their way of thinking."

Again, buoyed by her own courage and dreamer's fearless attitude, Juliet moved straight ahead, eventually opening her second business—the Professional Massage Training Center, also in Springfield. Juliet is the school's director and one of its instructors. Since opening its doors, the Center has graduated approximately 100 students. There are usually 12 to 16 students per class, and each class lasts 8 to 10 months.

"Our students work mainly in hospitals," Juliet says. "We work with all types of patients—cancer patients, people in detox, people undergoing chemotherapy. We also work with athletes, but not in a hospital setting. It's very fulfilling to me to see the great work our students are doing."

Credibility is the backbone of any educational institution. Without it, success simply cannot be achieved. To not be credible is to not be taken seriously. Juliet's task, then, was to set about building credibility.

But how? The medical community is, as everyone knows, off limits to outsiders, difficult to penetrate and painfully slow to contemplate—much less accept—change. And now here came this little lady, a *massage therapist* of all things, espousing the benefits of alternative medicine. What *chutzpah!*

But when Juliet showed up at their door, she wasn't without her own weapons, namely the fine reputation she had carved out for herself over the previous 10 years.

"The connections I had established with the local medical community enabled me to overcome some of their early reservations," Juliet says. "Also, Springfield is a big medical city with some very bright people who see the value of non-invasive treatment. Their feeling is, 'OK, let's try it.' Plus, by having been here for 15 years, people know and trust me. They know that what we do really works."

Despite that, Juliet says the Center initially met with some reluctance. But much of that was laid to rest when one of the students wrote a prototype program, presented it and had it accepted. That program, Juliet proudly says, has become extremely popular.

The students train under the guidance of licensed therapists, then get their hands-on experience by doing volunteer work at local hospitals. The excellent work by the students is another reason why the Center was able to establish almost instant credibility.

"There really could be no doubting us once people saw what our students were doing, and the great results they were getting," Juliet says. "It's hard for anyone to argue against success."

The Professional Massage Training Center, once seen as an outlaw upstart, is now approved by the Coordinating Board of Higher Education in Missouri, the same governing body that approves all post-high school education.

Clearly, Juliet's baby has come of age.

And the future looks even brighter.

"Only now are we beginning to open our eyes in this country to the possibilities alternative medicines bring," she says. "We work with all different sorts of medicines—Eastern, Chinese, Vietnamese. And in Europe, CAM (complementary and alternative medicine) is a standard part of their approach to healing. I don't think we have to look too far off into the future before that will be true in the United States as well."

After having waged so many hard-fought battles, one can't help but wonder: Has she managed to maintain her rebellious entrepreneur's spirit?

The answer to that is a resounding yes.

"My basic philosophy is fairly simple," Juliet says. "Entrepreneurs, employers and employees gain much more when they engage themselves in operating businesses that are profitable and efficient. As everyone's needs and goals are addressed within the group structure, you create an environment that serves workers, their families and the community."

Juliet admits to being a workaholic. That is, until recently.

"I worked constantly," she says. "All the time. With the exception of doing work for the church, virtually all of my time was spent on the job. I really enjoyed it, but it had almost become all-consuming. But when my father got ill, it helped me put things in perspective. I started taking some time for myself, going boating or to ball games. Just learning how to relax a little."

If you ask Juliet to assess her accomplishments, she will quickly point out the two she's most proud of—that she succeeded at such a young age ("Only now am I starting to realize how young I am to have done what I've done.") and that she did it without any outside financial help.

That's right. Juliet and banks have never been on speaking terms.

"I've never taken a bank loan for any of my businesses," she says, adding with a laugh, "mainly because banks didn't want anything to do with us. We were way too much of a risk for them. We support ourselves with money from tuition, product sales, continuing education, things like that. So far, no bank money has been involved."

Well, surprise. After our talk, Juliet phoned back a couple of weeks later with news. She hired a new business partner skilled in organizing, and the partner brought a bank on board—a big step toward reaching their goal of making the Professional Massage Training Center *the* center for teaching complementary and alternative medicine.

"If everything goes well, it should take about five years for us to really make a name for ourselves," she says.

Things are already starting to roll. Juliet was appointed by Governor Mel Carnahan to the first Missouri Board for Massage Therapy as its educational representative. The action allows the state to license massage therapists and come in line with national standards.

And what will she do if more obstacles get in her path? The same as she's always done.

"I just try to become like water and flow around it," she says. "Let the stone wall be and just do what you have to do. That's what I've always done. I'll go through a period of evaluation, asking myself if this is what I really want to do. Is it me? Once I say yes, then I set up a strategy, a plan of attack. And then I go after it."

A CONVERSATION WITH JULIET MEE . . .

As a kid, who other than your parents did you look up to?

I received a lot of my role modeling from my teachers while I was in elementary school. Two teachers who were extremely important to me were Mrs. Barker, my first grade teacher, and Mrs. Marabel, my fifth grade teacher.

Mrs. Barker was the first person I remember (outside of my family) who treated me as if there was something sparkly and spectacular about me. She called all of us girls "Lady" and taught us that who we were and how we acted was important. She was quick to praise me, but she didn't let me off the hook if I did something that was unacceptable. She brought beauty into our lives in many ways, but specifically with a project we all participated in where we watched the metamorphosis of a caterpillar into a butterfly. She filled us with a love for learning and for beauty.

Mrs. Marabel taught us how to do our basic work quickly, accurately and creatively. I am a very competitive person, so what I learned from her was how to have a friendly competition with my classmates that ended up producing a fun time for all of us.

What about early influences from the entrepreneurial perspective?

Much of that came from baby-sitting for people who had their own business. They were very influential because they let me see what it was like to own and operate your own business. They also explained to me why you would want to be the one in charge, and what responsibilities were involved in running a business. It was just a wonderful learning experience.

Later, when I was 16, two people I baby-sat for, Tom and Pam Pierson, hired me to work in their business. It was called Kaleidoscope. They sold exotic gifts, and it was considered a "cool" place. It was a small store, but people were always waiting in line to get in. Tom and Pam taught me many things, first and foremost the importance of treating people with respect. They were also quick to tell you how important you were, not only to the store but to them. I doubt if either of them ever read a book on business management. But it didn't matter. They knew what excellent customer service was. That's why their store thrived in Springfield for 25 years.

Tom and Pam watched over me and never let me forget what was important during a time when I could have gotten wild and out of control. They treated me with respect, but most important, they believed that I had something within me that was worthwhile, something I should be proud of. Their encouragement was essential to my growth as a person and an entrepreneur.

Obviously, you're something of an outsider. What's it like to be perceived that way, rightly or wrongly?

My situation is unique. I was, and am, an outsider in that part of the world that I regularly move in. However, I have a tremendous amount of support in other parts of my life, support from family and friends who love me and understand what I am doing. Without their support, I don't believe I could do all the things I've done.

The situations where I feel like an outsider are when I'm in the medical field, the financial world of banking and the mainstream world of business. Many times, when I'm in those worlds, I've felt like I was attending a party that I'd been invited to by mistake. Now, though, when that happens, I show up and act as if I have every right to be there.

What's the secret to being a successful entrepreneur?

It requires an odd mix of personal characteristics. By its very nature, it takes a person who is comfortable with risk. However, an entrepreneur has to be adept at maintaining relationships with family and friends who are not comfortable with the risks you are taking. To be successful, you must have the right mix of talent and perseverance.

OK, which do you think is more important, talent or perseverance?

In the long run, I'd say perseverance is more important. You must continue on with your ideas and plans even in those situations when no one agrees with your vision. Entrepreneurial visionaries are probably the bravest people I know.

Why do you say that?

Because when you are ahead of your time, it is extremely difficult to deal with all of the issues related to business while at the same time trying to create a new path. Usually there are very few institutions who are willing to loan you money. To them, dreams aren't sound collateral. So, unless the entrepreneurial visionary has his own money, he can be in for a lot of agonizing times.

It helps tremendously to have that odd internal sense of timing that tells you when to move and when to sit. That's an important element to cultivate within yourself, because common sense won't work when you are dealing with true risks.

Now that you have employees, how have those early experiences influenced the way you manage people?

I was 28 when I hired my first employee. I had never worked within a group office environment. I imagined a perfect world where everyone knew how to work together without practice or a plan. In fact, I thought policies and procedures stifled creativity, and that articulating what needed to be done was insulting. I thought we could all just do what needed to be done for the day and that responsibilities could easily be kept to a minimum. I didn't understand that my employees were supposed to make money for me as well as for themselves.

I became tremendously overwhelmed and was too embarrassed to tell the employees that I couldn't do all my therapies, manage the office, do promotions, do the scheduling and clean the toilets, too. I loved my business, my service and my employees. Unfortunately, I ended up becoming a martyr who thought I was the only one doing things right, that I was the only one contributing. Needless to say, that wasn't the case. I was the problem, the creator of the chaos. Consequently, it was up to me to change the way I did things. I almost lost my businesses due to my well-intentioned ignorance.

Since those days, I have learned a tremendous amount about compassion, about leading people in a compassionate way, and what types of direction people need and want. I now know how to give employees a feeling that they have a stake in the outcome. I know my boundaries and theirs. So I guess I worked the plan backwards and now understand about good business and leadership practices.

How important is it that the people you work with share your dream or vision?

From just a practical standpoint, if they don't share my dreams and visions and see their place within that picture, they need to get onto their own true path. That doesn't mean I'm a tyrant who says "It's my way or the highway." In fact, if I err in my management style, it is in consulting too much and directing too little. But if someone has a serious resistance to the big picture, they need to leave as soon as possible. The environment will not be good for anyone once we have identified the split. However, my ideology is a little different in this regard. I do not see someone as being wrong when they have a big difference of opinion. Rather, I see it as their life's path emerging.

Was it difficult to get workers with similar attitudes to yours?

No. Most of my employees went to my massage school before I hired them, so I had seen their work habits and attitudes for 8 to 10 months. The ones who have not attended my school came to me because they believe in the way we do business and in the direction our company is going.

When dealing with risks, how do you stay true to your goals and not let the fear of failure derail you?

I've thought that I was right for so long that I can't remember even considering not being true to my goals. My life opened up when I dropped fear and began to teach my ideas about the way that the world, medicine, business and life could be. I understand that it is just fine to do a great big belly flop, to fail, or to not reach my goal, just as long as I tried my best. I wake up every day looking for the adventure and knowing it will be there.

You faced intense skepticism when you first started out. Did you ever doubt?

I think you are nuts if you don't have doubts. Your doubts are the waves upon your ship that make you look at the compass and re-evaluate the path you've chosen.

What gave you the internal sense that the time was right to go out on your own?

I got the message to move into my office when I couldn't accommodate the number of clients I had. I got the message to teach when I couldn't find anyone to hire. I once asked a favorite client if he had any business advice for me. He gave me the best advice ever. He said, "When you don't know what to do, don't do anything. Sit back and trust that the answer will come to you."

We all know when it's time to move. It's just that we procrastinate or stay where we are until someone forces us to move. You just get better at hearing the voice and acting upon it. What used to take me months now takes me moments. Saving time is important, so I have learned to listen carefully.

Is being in touch with that internal sense essential to holding onto dreams in the face of difficulty?

That gut-level, intuitive sense is your connection to God, the world and other people. It is your direction during a business deal as well as your protection on a dark street. It is imperative that we use it, and not just in times of difficulty.

You faced intense opposition and lack of support from city officials when you started out. What was the worst point during those days?

There was so much misunderstanding about the regulation of skilled touch that the previous rules and regulations really didn't pertain to the type of work we were doing at our school. The worst point in dealing with the people who had control of the regulation of training and licensing of massage therapists was the meeting where they showed me who was in charge.

Neither of us wanted to give up our position. I thought that we could reach some sort of win-win solution, but that's not what happened. The decision given to me was not fair, and actually punitive to my students, my school and me. But what doesn't kill you makes you stronger.

Before that incident, I was naïve to what powerful people can do. That evening, I felt empty, without my previous beliefs in what justice and fair treatment meant. But overnight, the emptiness became an iron resolve to succeed. And I have.

What helped you the most in not abandoning your dream during that period?

I had wonderful friends who consulted with me daily as if I was on a survival mission. They took my late-night phone calls and seemed to genuinely care about the incidents that were going on. They believed that this wasn't about an ordinance, it was about making a difference in the system. They told me that somebody had to do it, and that I was the only one who might survive because I had been born and raised in the community and because of my strong clientele of influential people.

What did you learn about yourself—and other people— when overcoming obstacles?

That I have what it takes to do whatever needs to be done, even though I might not get it done until the last minute. No one does much of anything alone, so it is vital to cultivate good friends and business allies. I figured out that it is OK to take a stand even if no one agrees with you. I have learned to love people who are taking a stand that I do not agree with. I have learned that no one stops you, that you stop yourself.

Where do you see the future of alternative medicine heading?

I believe that complementary and alternative medicine will be used first in many chronic and acute medical conditions. It is often the least invasive, safest way to deal with a problem. If it doesn't work, then medication or surgery will be the next step.

It may be difficult to get people to understand wellness care at first. However, in the long run, it will save time and money. We also just can't afford the medicine we have had in the past. And more patients are unwilling to accept all the effects of conventional treatment.

Why do you think the United States is so reluctant to embrace the alternative approach?

I wish I had a different answer because this sounds so combative, but I feel that there has been a tremendous organized effort in mainstream medicine in the past. The AMA, the insurance companies and the pharmaceutical companies have tried to exclude and limit people's health care options, as well as to remove credibility from the results that patients report.

The Internet has made information so readily available that we are being allowed into the arena of health care on two fronts. The first—and most important of these—is that patients are requiring their health care team to do a better job of communicating. Also, patients no longer respect the boundaries or lines drawn in the sand between the two sides. They just want results.

The second factor is that there is a tremendous amount of money being spent on complementary and alternative medicine. The vast majority of that money is out-of-pocket expense that isn't reimbursed by insurance. That fact alone has made the health care industry sit up and notice us.

If you could change anything about yourself, or your approach to things, what would it be?

I wouldn't take things so seriously. I tend to act as if every thought, every comment, every move, every decision is life or death. I give other people tremendous latitude but very little to myself. I over-process and over-analyze my own behavior. I hold myself to ridiculous standards that are unattainable, or at least unattainable by me.

What problems can arise when you pass your "ridiculous standards" to those who work for you?

I ask people to do things when they are too tired. I ask people to make me their priority. I expect constant vigilance over what I see as being important details. I expect them to overlook my flaws and get rid of theirs.

How much has family support meant to you, especially during those darker times?

I am very close to my family and always have been. I have a big family, with three sisters and one brother, all of whom are married, two nieces and two nephews. I think my family has only now reached a point where they can give me practical support, such as sitting down with me and discussing my ideas, plans, businesses, and so on. They have never really been able to see what I knew was possible to achieve. It seemed to be in the realm of the impossible to them. However, my family has always been willing to support what I do unconditionally. They are always there for me. When I'm with them, I'm reminded of what is really important in life.

Is being something of a rebel almost a prerequisite to acting on dreams and turning them into reality?

I don't really think that most dreams are turned into reality through rebellion. I believe it happens because of a deep inner longing and a drive to make a difference in life. I think that deep within the dream is your highest potential.

If you had to advise others on the secret to turning dreams into success, what would you tell them?

Live your life as art. See beauty in your life and your dreams. Stretching your limits can be painful and even humbling, but it *is* worth it. In fact, attempting to fulfill your dreams is the only thing that really matters. Who cares if you fail at trying your dream? What matters is that you made the effort, that you gave it everything you have. That's what counts.

Bill Phifer left a successful corporate career to contemplate his life in a mountain cabin in upstate New York, then ventured to Lexington, Kentucky, and helped turn around Cosmo's specialty deli, finding his dream in the process.

12

BILL PHIFER
EATERY MANAGER,
"ACTIVITY TRAP" ESCAPEE

"Let your pendulum swing.
It will swing high and low, but God forbid it ever sits idle."

When we hired Bill Phifer to be general manager of Cosmo's Fine Foods, we felt we had the right man to activate one of our dreams—putting into practice the values and insights from our Lessons in Leadership® programs and making them thrive in the demanding world of retail food sales.

Cosmo's is a labor of love—a specialty food deli and eatery where we wanted the personality of the place to match the fun, enthusiasm and genuineness of the people who work there. But none of that was in place when Bill came along.

Little did we know then that in having Bill share our dream, his own dream was coming true. It's a dream that was born in darkness and doubt, but burns bright today. Still, the path to it was stalked by uncertainty.

Despite a highly successful career with a large corporation, Bill had become tangled up in the rush and stress of constant travel and endless problems that were his to solve. He did so admirably, but the grind was taking its toll. He had a career, but did he have a life? He wasn't so certain anymore. So, in a leap of faith, he quit his position, spent a year of soul-searching that sometimes reached despair and emerged, finally, with a decision to come from New York state to Lexington.

"It was a bungee jump," Bill says, "and I didn't know how long the cord was or how long the drop was going to be. But it was well worth the jump."

To say the least.

In little more than a year since joining Cosmo's, Bill has helped spark a successful rebirth. In the May 1999 issue of *Southern Living* magazine, Cosmo's was called "Lexington's coolest new eatery and grocery." The remarkable turnaround that Bill helped engineer—by raising morale (and profits) at a deli that was floundering under previous ownership—made him a subject of Stephen Covey's latest book, *Living the 7 Habits*.

But that's mostly the Cosmo's story. It doesn't begin to tell the whole story of Bill Phifer.

After a 23-year career that included a position as director of sales for one of the nation's largest specialty food companies, where he traveled a seven-state territory and oversaw almost 200 people and 1,500 retail accounts, Bill began to question everything.

"I decided that I'd had enough," he says. "Sometimes it's just as good to find out what you don't want as it is to find out what you do want. I decided to resign and change the course of my life."

He and his father had built a small cabin in upstate New York, between the Adirondacks and the Catskills. Living only an hour away in Albany, Bill would visit the place whenever he could. He'd fix the bathroom or the fireplace. He'd chop wood.

"I had no plans—none whatsoever," he says. "I was so caught up with what I had been doing in my job that it hadn't enabled me to think about what I really wanted to do, so I figured the best way was simply to sever all ties and just start with a clear head."

And so he'd go to the cabin. In those first months, the winter was harsh and gloomy. It matched Bill's mood. Often stranded in the cabin by a blizzard, he'd sit and reflect on a life that, to him, offered no clear picture. The days were dark. So were many of his thoughts.

"Very dark," he says. "It was a very deep well I was going through. It was almost as if I was in this state of hopelessness. But I remember my father once said that when you're bored, it means you're really capping something that's going to explode. So I hung in there. And finally I just said to myself, 'You know, things won't come to you. You're going to have to make things happen.'

"And it's true. You really are in control of what happens to you. By that I mean, I didn't know which way the road would curve, but I knew I had to at least get on the road and go down it rather than sit idle."

The work around the cabin helped. Wood chopping and puttering around the place awakened something in Bill. "I found that it was a definite change from the mental work I was used to," he says. "It gave me a chance to let my artistic and creative juices flow. It was good to get that release. And so, as that year went on, I found myself feeling real good about going up there."

After things became clearer, he decided he would leave Albany and come to Lexington. His sister had moved there to start an herb business, and his father had moved there as well. "I called them one day," he says, "and said, 'Guess what? I'm packin' up, I'm movin' out, and I'm on my way down.'"

He found an apartment and got some work with a local natural foods co-op, helping with purchasing. There he met Anne Hopkins, the general manager. Together they increased business by 40 percent in two years. Just about then, Cosmo's was starting up. Bill and Anne checked out the store, and wound up becoming consultants. Then they were hired full-time, with Bill becoming general manager.

Shortly after taking the position, he wondered if he'd made a huge mistake. Cosmo's was new in name and ownership and big on dreams, but the previous store had been in serious financial trouble with poor customer service, little leadership and lots of distrust and disillusion among employees.

In time, however, all that changed. Exposing employees to the teachings of leaders like Stephen Covey, Tom Peters, Ken Blanchard and Robert Cooper—but more important, practicing those values himself—Bill began to turn the dream into the success it's becoming today.

Cosmo's had a 32.2 percent gain in sales and a 46 percent gain in customer count in 1998. Salaries went up 14.5 percent, but the ratio of labor dollars to sales decreased by 17.67 percent. In that same year, the store eliminated a $45,000 per month deficit and now operates in the black.

Bill Phifer could never have imagined where his path would lead him. He merely recognized that something was missing and sought to fill the void. His path wasn't clear, nor were the solutions. He simply set out with his dream, and it collided with ours.

We should all have such happy accidents.

A CONVERSATION WITH BILL PHIFER . . .

You left a successful career and plunged into the unknown. Looking back, what was telling you that you needed a change?

You know, the perks were there. There was everything, but I just wasn't gratified. I felt as though there's got to be more. It's just not enough to make a good paycheck. You have to feel as though you've accomplished something. You have to get feedback. Plus, I really felt that after doing it for 23 years, being in distribution for various companies, I wanted to see what other options were there for me. I knew there were other things I wanted to try. I wanted to try to fill that pie more, if that's a way to describe it. I had a lot of versatility in the job I had, but the gratification wasn't there any more. It was getting to be very unrewarding.

How so?

Well, in this day and age it's very fast paced. My job was very bottom line-oriented. I'm a people person, and I also like a lot of creative thinking where you can try things and you can experiment. There wasn't a whole lot of that where I was. I think just the fast pace alone . . . I realized that, wow, I was going so fast that I didn't have time to look to the right or left.

What was a typical week like for you?

Oh, gosh. I had a responsibility over seven states. I had a couple hundred people within those seven states. My typical week would be everything from south New Jersey to Buffalo, New York, and then getting over to Pennsylvania. Flights, driving. A tremendous amount of traveling. A lot of overnight stays in hotels.

People tend to think, "Wow, what a wonderful life," but after awhile you realize you have no foundation. You go home merely to change your clothes and get back out on the road again. But I love to work. I know people say, "Well, you have to be half out of your mind." But I've always liked to keep very active.

Well, that's the irony, isn't it? It's not the work per se. It's just whether it's consuming you and not allowing you to live a full life.

Yes, exactly. It's balance. It's all about balance. And I finally came to an age where wisdom started to set in, and it said, "Wait a minute. There's another half of you that you haven't even gotten to know yet. Why don't you go find yourself?"

It was funny. The company I'd worked for, great company. I was very fortunate to be able to be a part of that, but at the same time I looked around and said, "Well, wait one minute here. There's more. There's more."

It seems that in bigger companies, even if the intentions are good, often there's just not enough time to implement things you'd like to do because there's so much work.

I think it was a matter of being in a very reactive type of business rather than pro-active. And my job really involved a lot of troubleshooting. When you're in that state, you're constantly putting out fires. And my ultimate goal was not to be the Michael Jordan of Fixit. I think it's great that I was part of a team. We worked hard. But at the same time, it was a very reactive type of situation I was in.

It's interesting how dreams can materialize out of the blue, once you set out on a path. You say you wanted to be more creative, and suddenly you wind up in Lexington, and suddenly you're at Cosmo's where Larry says, "Here's what I'm looking for." And it's the very thing you wanted. When we talked with Joanne Everett, she said she couldn't explain a lot of things in her life, that it was almost as if the hand of God was playing chess. Can you see that in your story, too?

Yes, and it's funny, you know? When you're going through it, you're scared to death. You're saying, "I've let go of the very last thing I've got any anchor to"—which was my job, being that I had no family to speak of. Because of all my traveling, I was constantly busy, and to suddenly have this void . . .

But it was a void I needed in order to re-create myself. And it *is* funny. It's almost as though things just work out. Still, it was a very scary time, and it was a very lonely time. It was a time of a lot of apprehension. But when you have to dig deep, it's fascinating what will come out. Although it was a painful experience, it was well worth it.

That's another common thread we're finding. When we ask what's the biggest thing that stops people from going after their dreams, they almost invariably say it's fear.

Well, I'm a big believer in dreams. Basically I'm a curious person. I love curious people. I love people who wonder why. I have a lot of dreams and I enjoy dreaming. And so that plays a big role in some of the things I do. And I'm living a dream right now, to some degree. But now, out of that comes another dream. The dreams just keep building on each other.

I'm not going to sit here and tell you I'm a spiritual person or anything else. But there is, I think, some sort of bigger power that helps to steer us down the road. I definitely got some sort of spiritual experience out of the whole thing.

We've discovered that, if you commit to a path—even if you're not entirely sure what that path is—things start to happen. Help appears, and it pops up in unexpected places.

Well, you know, I think back on my younger years. Charles Kurault was one of my idols. I always liked his "On the Road" shows. They were almost a philosophy about life. He would just get in that bus and ride around the country and have all these new experiences. I've always admired that, and always said to myself, "Boy, I'd love to live that kind of life, where you never know what's around the bend, but when you go around it, it usually turns out to be a real good turn."

What's the next dream for you?

I think it's to get even more of a foundation to what I'm doing. I've been down here now for awhile. I've settled in somewhat. I'd certainly like to have a family and things I didn't have in the past. A lot of it was my lifestyle.

Have you been single all your life?

Yes, all my life. I guess you could say it was for a lot of reasons, but I think a lot of it was that I was so consumed by my work. That's another side of that balance I mentioned earlier, where I was so caught up with what I was doing in that "activity trap," as I call it. I never stepped out and looked in. And I think leaving that job gave me a chance to sit in the bleachers and look down at the field and say, "What's really going on here?" I'll tell you, being a spectator isn't all that bad.

In terms of balance, it's not only important to have it internally as a leader, but you've also got to strike that balance with the people you're leading. You've got a bottom line consideration, but you've also got to create the climate where they're empowered to dream, to act on things.

Oh yeah. I think, in fact, that Cosmo's has almost been a haven where we've collectively gotten together and had these dreams, and we do our dream comparisons. I mean, how often is it that you can say in the workplace that you get a chance to sit around with a bunch of people and talk about what your dreams are, rather than just bottom line? I think that kind of culture and that kind of atmosphere makes people more excited about what they're doing.

I've been very fortunate to be with a group of people who have a wide variety of talents and backgrounds and dreams here. And just the fact we could sit and share these things has made it a great place to work. So this is a team effort. And the odd thing is that none of us really have a lot in common, other than that we're curious people and we're all just trying to better our lives.

What's the key to creating the right atmosphere?

I think it's to constantly expand your way of thinking, to constantly accept new ways of thinking. I've learned so much from listening to other people. You know, I come from what would be considered a fairly regimented background where there were a lot of perimeters. And yet, here it's this creative mode that we're always in. I really enjoy that. It's been great.

When we first told you that's the kind of "feel" we wanted, were you skeptical?

No, quite the contrary. I think I've always had that belief in trust, of letting people make things happen. But with that comes accountability and responsibility. But I have to tell you that it got me excited to hear you say, "You do whatever you think."

One of my dreams, of course, when I left the larger corporation was that I just wanted to be myself. I knew there were a lot of things that I hadn't tapped into. And here you were telling me, "Do whatever you think. We have complete faith and trust in what you're going to do."

I'm surrounded by people who have that same feeling here in the store. There's a lot of trust. And we *do* disagree. I love that. I don't like to be around "yes people."

Well, if you don't allow that atmosphere to exist where people can speak their mind, you start having resentments develop under the surface that can really sabotage things.

Oh, sure. I really believe that when we disagree, the best things come out of it. I've learned a lot from the people around me, merely because they've disagreed with me on many things and I wind up agreeing with them. I think if you can keep that mutual respect for each other's thoughts and opinions—but do it in a way that's creative, it's wonderful. It's a great way to be.

You faced a lot of problems here at first. How did you juggle all of that and not lose sight of doing it the right way?

I think my own impatience was my biggest battle. But that was part of the change, that was part of the reason I'm here, I think. Not only for working with Cosmo's, but for myself—to learn how to be better all around, to be a thinker and how to take a completely different approach to things.

So I really listened and I observed and I watched. People gave me a lot of insight as to what needed to be done. I merely tried to bring to the table my "toolbox" and say, "Here are some tools that might help you." They've done the rest. It's just that I was there to say, "Have you tried this size wrench? This might fit better." And I think that suddenly people felt that they were being heard. They got very enthusiastic about it.

There was a comment one fellow said the other day. He said, "You know, I came to work here and the first meeting, you all scared the hell out of me because I didn't think you knew what you were doing—because you let me talk the entire time."

But then, he said, "Suddenly I realized that, no, the whole thing was that you were giving me my chance to have my say in what's going on. I realized how smart that was."

I think it's a shock to a lot of people that they're in this kind of environment, where we're really interested in what you have to say, regardless of how far out it sounds. And the more you do that, the more people take hold of things and say, "I have a piece of this, and this is important to me."

So, again, I go back to thinking that, yes, I was overwhelmed at first. I was thinking, "Wow, where do I start?" Well, it's that first step. You start there. And that's really what it's been all about.

Your story about the new employee thinking that the company was without direction because he was allowed to talk is revealing. It shows just how strong the attitude is in a lot of companies, where everybody has come to regard it as normal to sit mute and just hear edicts from above.

Yes, and both of you have practiced what you've preached. You've been extremely supportive of what we're trying to do here, rather than being authoritative or trying to dictate how we should run the business. I'm also trying to do that with our employees. You know, it's so important to catch people doing things right. There are plenty of places at work where everybody is going to catch you doing the wrong thing.

"Catching people doing things right" is one of Ken Blanchard's favorite lines, and you obviously have the same attitude. When you first came to Cosmo's, you really didn't know about the involvement with Lessons in Leadership and people like Dr. Blanchard. Yet what they preach is what you seem to have always wanted to practice. Just another example of synchronicity.

And isn't it funny, isn't it ironic—because here I was, thinking that the only way I'm ever going to get into that kind of atmosphere is to do it myself. And yet I find somebody else who has the same dream.

What you said about learning that you needed more patience reminds us of what somebody once said: The universe keeps sending you the lesson until you learn it.

Exactly, exactly! And I believe I've had a lot of repeated messages in my life.

Well, we all have.

Right. But I think I'm getting the message now. You know, one of the other things I've enjoyed about this job goes back to when I was a kid. Remember when you were given the instruction book along with the bicycle? I'm not really good at sitting there and just reading the instructions. I need to visualize and then try to put it together without the instructions. So I surround myself now with people who know how to read instructions, and we complement each other that way. That's helped me through the tough moments.

You know, I think we're on a different train. There's a lot of people where I came from, they're getting on the train going out, not coming in. And I think a lot of people are starting to realize that, "Wait a minute, there's a different approach. There's a different way." It doesn't have to be 80-hour weeks. The quality of work you do and how much you enjoy it is more important.

In the long run, it's not productive to push people that hard?

I don't believe it is, because you slowly begin to back out of your productive mode when you get to the point where you can't even think any more because you've put in so much time. But there's a fine line between burnout and enthusiasm. I find here that some of the staff just hang out to help with things even when they're not on the clock, and that tells me, wow, they've taken hold of this thing.

If you had to advise somebody on how to turn dreams into success, what would you tell them?

Go with your gut. Go with your instincts. Trust yourself. And realize that everything has its risks. But let your pendulum swing. It will swing high and low, but God forbid it ever sits idle. Let it swing, and you'll be surprised how many good things will happen to you, how many great people you'll meet. It really is a great thing to go for it. Just go for it.

And many of those dreams will come true.

Oh, yes. I still talk to some of the people I used to work with, and I see that nothing has changed in their lives. That's sad to me. My road could just as well have gone bad. I guess I could have had some sort of catastrophe, but I was willing to take that chance, because it was so important to me to make a change and to find out more about myself. Maybe that's selfish, but I wanted to find out a little more about what my wants and needs were.

Well, that's not really selfish. You can't be a good leader—
or be able to pursue your dreams—unless you take time to
discover those things.

And you know, it's funny—I'm crossing paths with other
people who have done the same thing. And I have yet to meet
somebody who said, "Boy, did I make a big mistake!"

Another dreamer, Willie King, told us that he's had disas-
ters, but after getting through each one, it proved to be the
best thing that could have happened.

Yes. Even during those times back in the mountains when I
was feeling down and out and lonely and in the middle of snow-
storms and cold and all of that, there was a reason for it. Because
the sun was about to shine.

Joanna McGoldrick, with son Bill, son-in-law Andrew and daughter Beth Ann; and getting around on her own in a life remarkable for the independent spirit she's maintained.

13

JOANNA MCGOLDRICK
STUDENT, ADVENTURER,
MS "VICTOR"

"You have to explore the possibilities.
Sometimes you have to jump through hoops."

For six months, the motorized scooter sat mostly unused in the corner of Joanna McGoldrick's living room in Las Vegas. Only on rare occasions—on long shopping trips to the mall, for example—would she use it. The scooter became her foe, a symbol of defeat in the battle she was waging to live the life of independence she dreamed of.

She stuck with her cane and walker, even as the multiple sclerosis (MS) that was breaking down the sheath protecting her nerves made it increasingly difficult to use her left arm and left leg. Her innate resolve and determination, which had served her well as she negotiated the challenges of living with MS, would, in this instance, literally lead to her downfall. Despite both aids, she kept falling—fracturing her ankle, rupturing her spleen and, finally, breaking her hip. That last fall not only forced her into the scooter but made it necessary for nurse's aides to come to her home each morning and evening to help her in and out of bed. She resented them. To her, the aides heralded the arrival of a day she had long dreaded—the day when she would become a burden, an object of pity.

But out of those angry, resentful days, Joanna emerged with a new outlook on independence, viewing it in a way she had never before considered. Joanna had always believed her independence would be compromised if she leaned on others for support. Instead, she found it was strengthened and nurtured through others' assistance.

She learned a lesson we all eventually stumble upon as we sleepwalk through the early steps of a dream—that in achieving our dreams, even ones of independence, the aid of others is always required. Joanna eventually welcomed her aides, looking forward to their visits and the new alliances and bonds she developed. "I have met some extremely wonderful women, so caring, and have become friends with many of them," she says.

She began to use the scooter, finding that instead of limiting her, it transported her to a new level of freedom. "When I was forced to use it, I realized how much better my life was because I wasn't so tired and because it gave me more freedom," she says.

Today, 21 years after being diagnosed with MS, Joanna has managed to attain a remarkable level of independence. Her life is a daily demonstration to others that our lives—and our dreams—might sometimes take a detour, but that the alternate route is often filled with experiences that can make it as rewarding as the main road.

In 1978, Joanna was a 44-year-old mother of two with a troubled marriage and a lingering pinched feeling in her leg. The marriage eventually dissolved. The pinched feeling didn't. When it was diagnosed as MS, the news that she had a crippling disease for which there is no cure was devastating to her—as it would be to any of us. "I just wanted to go into the bedroom and shut the door," she told the *Las Vegas Review-Journal* in an interview several years ago.

That comment seems completely out of character for the woman you meet today, a woman who crosses out the word "victim" in stories that refer to her as a multiple sclerosis victim. Indeed, victor is more like it. At age 65, Joanna still rises at 5 A.M. to be at her desk each weekday in the Division of Continuing Education at the University of Nevada-Las Vegas, where she is a management assistant. She's worked for the university for 22 years—and for the past 25 years she has been slowly, methodically working her way toward the college degree she has longed for since she was 18. When we talked with her, she was just two classes away from graduation. That dusty old dream will come true in May 2000.

"A long time ago," Joanna says, "a friend told me, 'There are people to meet, places to go and things to do.' Well, it might take me a little longer, but I'll still get there."

She's been getting there all along. In the 1980s, she launched three home-based sales businesses to give herself a little more income and to meet new people. In 1984, she was chosen second runner-up as Handicapped Worker of the Year in Nevada. In 1989, based on her poise and personality, she was crowned Ms. Wheelchair Nevada and competed for Ms. Wheelchair America in Mobile, Alabama.

Through the years, she's traveled from coast to coast each year to visit family in Connecticut, Massachusetts and California. In recent years, even after she became confined to a scooter, she rode horseback and went water skiing just to prove she could.

"I'm always game for a new adventure," she says.

If her life has a theme, she says, it would be that love for adventure. Joanna has always sought it. But growing up in Meriden, Connecticut, she sometimes found her wings clipped by overly protective parents. It was the 1950s, as she points out, a different era for women. College was considered a luxury, not a necessity. And choices were limited. Women weren't encouraged to seek many career paths other than teaching, nursing or secretarial work.

In fact, her lack of interest in teaching or nursing caused her parents to decide she did not need to go to college. "My parents asked me if I wanted to be a schoolteacher or a nurse, and I said no," she says. "So they insisted I take secretarial classes."

She lived at home, surrounded by family—her first generation Italian-American parents, four siblings and a network of aunts, uncles and cousins who lived within shouting distance. She worked as an executive and legal secretary, went to the beach on weekends, dated, bought a car—a two-year-old '57 Chevy, black and white with silver fins and a red interior, she remembers fondly—and took some wonderful trips with friends to Nassau, Bermuda, Puerto Rico and Las Vegas. In 1958, two of her friends went to California and stayed. When she told her mother she'd like to do the same, Joanna says, "My mother would go into hysterics." And so, rather than cause family upheaval, she continued to live at home and work.

"My family gave me solid values. Everybody had mothers and fathers who were married and stayed married and it was very close-knit. But I felt smothered," Joanna says. "I always wanted to go away, but I never had the gumption to do it. I don't know if I was lazy or it was the MS in the background. I just kind of let things happen instead of making things happen."

At 30, she married a hometown boy who had been out West, working at casinos in Reno. They moved to Las Vegas so he could work at the casinos there, and for the first time Joanna found herself away from everything and everyone familiar. She worked for a while, had a daughter, then a son, became a stay-at-home mom and moved to her dream home, complete with pool. She was living the 1950s dream of marriage: husband, two kids, a home and, as Joanna says, "living happily ever after. I was extremely happy."

To make the picture even brighter, at the urging of her husband Joanna began taking classes at UNLV in 1974. "I went to UNLV and registered for English and history," she says. "They were requirements. I absolutely fell in love with school. All I wanted to do was come home and study and have the rest of the world go away."

Slowly though, her dream life began to unravel. She and her husband separated. She decided to go to work and found a job at the university. The couple reunited and then Joanna learned she had MS. A few years later, they divorced.

Joanna became a working single parent, while dealing with a progressive illness that would gradually rob her of the use of her left arm and leg. "During the early years, I felt totally inadequate as a mother and was devastated thinking my kids were being cheated," she says. "However, I managed to drive them to every activity—soccer, baseball, basketball, movies, roller skating, dance lessons, Girl Scouts. They did not miss a single activity."

She must have done some pretty good parenting, despite her concerns. She raised two responsible, independent children, who both now live in California. Beth Ann, 33, is an actuary and lives in Los Angeles with her husband; Bill, 31, is a musician in Sacramento. Her children have been of utmost importance in her life, and now that they are adults, they have become her champions. "My children are my biggest supporters," she says. In recent years, she's focused on maintaining her freedom and independence by making her life as simple and uncomplicated as possible. Two important aspects of her life are her job at the university and the classes she has been taking there.

Carrol Steedman, director of the continuing education program, has worked closely with Joanna for almost two decades. Joanna answers questions and solves problems that pop up among the 18,000 class registrations the program handles each year. When students find themselves entangled in bureaucracy, "Joanna's the one light that finds a way for you to get things straightened out," says Carrol.

Working in a university setting is perfect for Joanna, who not only likes learning new skills on the job but relishes the challenges of the classroom. "What I enjoy about Joanna is that when she gets a chance to go to class with a good instructor, well, she is just in heaven," says Carrol. "She's really got a life of the mind."

While Joanna might be easygoing, she is definitely not a weak person. "I guess we could blame it on the Sicilians; I think they are known to be a sturdy lot," Carrol says with a quick laugh, referring to Joanna's Italian heritage.

"Joanna is very determined, with a wry sense of humor, very much her own person," Carrol says. "She's got a temperament where she can be diplomatic and say things the right way, but if anybody crosses the line, whether it's with sentiment, pity or stupidity, she'll just sort of cut it short. I never think of Joanna as a victim. I think of her as somebody who has learned a great deal and who has a lot of gumption to get the work done and done well."

Using the organizational skills and tenacity required daily in her job, Joanna has created systems that make her life easier to manage, giving herself more freedom in the process.

She hires others to clean, and when she shops, it's at a one-stop place like a mall. As much of her business as possible is done by mail. She's beginning to look at ways the computer could aid her. She works out arrangements with small businesses, like her dry cleaners, where staff come out to her car to pick up and deliver cleaning to her. A tenant eases the financial pressure of her condo mortgage and helps around the house. After a year of dealing with paperwork, state agencies and car dealers, she is about to get a new minivan equipped with a lift that will allow her to come and go as she pleases. Her current vehicle requires her to have assistance getting in and out.

And she's pondering her next dream, to live near the ocean—perhaps in California near her children—when she retires.

"I'd give anything to retire near the ocean, with my books and old movies," she says. "But that would still not be enough. I'd need to be near a college because I plan to always be a student." When she thinks back to what spurred her resolve to live life on her own terms—without, as she says, "someone hovering over me"—she remembers two conversations clearly.

The first made her angry—and more determined than ever. "When I found out I had MS, I went to a doctor in Santa Barbara, a neurosurgeon," she says, "and I will never forget sitting there looking at him as he told me, 'A third of people with MS do fine, a third are really bad and a third are in between. Some day, though, you might not be able to take care of yourself.' I left there and I was so mad. It was like he was giving me a death sentence."

The second was a conversation she had with her brother during a brief move back to Connecticut with her children when her marriage was in trouble. She was looking for support and connection and came to realize that though her family and friends cared about her, they had their own lives and problems. "My brother said to me, 'You know, you are alone,'" she recalls. "He was trying to tell me that nobody's going to take care of me, that I would have to stand up and take care of myself."

A CONVERSATION WITH JOANNA MCGOLDRICK . . .

You lost a lot with MS, but what do you think you gained from dealing with it these last two decades?

I think I gained a sense of empathy toward other people, not only the handicapped, but people of other colors and races, people with any kind of problem or who are dealing with general prejudice. Also, patience. I always was patient, and I guess it was a good thing.

Your independence is so important to you now, yet you say that independence wasn't a major theme in your life until you were diagnosed with MS.

Growing up in a large Italian family—I was the oldest of five children—we were very sheltered. My dad was very domineering.

Children were seen but not heard. My parents made every decision for us. We were not allowed to think, so growing up it was hard to be independent.

When I moved to Las Vegas, being away from my close family and many, many friends, I had to learn to be more independent. And then, independence became more important after MS. My life changed completely. I worked so hard to remain independent because I did not want to feel I was a burden to anyone.

Having parents who didn't support you in your dream to go to college—and who didn't allow you to make your own decisions and make your own mistakes—really affected your style as a parent, didn't it?

Yes. When my own daughter reached age 18, I encouraged her to go away to school. I did the same for my son. I wanted them to lead their own lives. I knew how it had affected me when I was kind of held back. Another reason was that I had MS and I didn't want them to stay here and feel they had to take care of me—and resent me.

You said that when you were younger, you sort of let things happen. Now you have a more assertive approach. What caused this change in your approach to life and to the things you want out of life?

When I was younger, there wasn't a need for me to do anything because everything in my life was in place. But when I was faced with MS, I thought, "What can I do to help make it go away or get better?" So I started checking out books at the library, reading everything I could get my hands on about MS. Instead of falling apart, I went to MS meetings. I joined discussion groups and met people, keeping as busy as possible. You have to find out yourself what you can do to help yourself. No one is going to drop into your living room and say, "Here is what you need." One of my professors told me you need to do something intellectually, and I've been taking classes ever since.

When you were faced with the news that you had MS, where did you find support?

At first I was embarrassed, afraid and mortified. I talked to a friend who told me, "You are just going to have to find your inner strength and pray." Someone told me about a prayer group, some ladies who met and prayed every day. I didn't know any of them, but it was a good place to go cry every morning and be safe and not cry in front of my children, my family or at work. I had grown up Catholic, where you say your prayers and hope for the best. That prayer group really helped.

My doctor also recommended I go to occupational rehabilitation. There they asked me, "What do you have trouble with." I said, "When I drop something on the floor, I can't reach it." So they ordered me this tool that is sort of a reacher. Then I told them, "I can't butter toast." Since I can't use my left hand, I can't hold the bread. So they ordered me a cutting board with a square on it to hold the toast.

It takes a lot of patience and perseverance to get the tools and assistance you need to live your dream of being as independent as possible.

To get these things through occupational rehabilitation, I had to go places and take tests. A lot of people wouldn't want to be bothered with it, but you can't have that kind of attitude. You have to explore the possibilities. Sometimes you have to jump through hoops and fill out papers. A lot of people I've come into contact with hear about these things and say, "Well, I'm not going to do that." But it isn't going to drop in your lap.

You've had to be patient to deal with various governmental systems for everything from health care to rehabilitation. This can often be frustrating.

Oh yes, I do get frustrated. But never enough to give up.

How has your attitude and dream of independence affected others?

I met this woman who was also in a wheelchair, and she found out that I had traveled by plane to Connecticut and California and she said, "Oh, you are so brave." And I said, "No I'm not. Anyone who can talk can fly." She called me later and said, "Guess what? I flew to California. I figured that if you could do it, I could do it."

There was another woman I knew, and she had MS, too. She didn't work; she drew social security. She always thought: "If I start working, I'll lose my social security, and why should I work and make a little when I could collect social security and not have to work?" But I was always working, and I would go to MS meetings and see her.

Well, one day she called me up and said, "Guess what. I got a job with the state. And I can't believe it, now I realize why you like working so much. I'm so happy. I love going to work." She had no idea. You just don't hear many people saying that, but it gives her a new purpose and meaning to life.

Most people live their lives waiting to retire—or waiting for it to be Friday or five o'clock. I think back on a girl who worked down the hall from me who was fighting cancer for years and years. She was given six months to live; then a month. Then she died. And now, when I hear others who worked with her wishing it was Friday I think, "I bet Jane—that's not her real name—wouldn't care what day or time it was if she could be here. MS has given me a different outlook on life. Instead of moaning that it is Monday and waiting for Friday to come, instead of wishing my life away, I'm living in the moment, rather than in the future. A lot of people live in the future or the past instead of the present. I just feel so fortunate to be here.

After you were diagnosed with MS, you went water skiing—using a board instead of skis—and you rode horseback. Why?

I gained self-confidence. I probably wouldn't have tried those things if I weren't handicapped, because I wouldn't have needed to prove myself. I think it was more for myself, though, to prove I'm not afraid and that I'm like everybody else.

You've worked full time, even after you were diagnosed with MS and even though the disease's progression has steadily made it more difficult for you to get around. Why have you always worked?

I feel better about myself; I've always wanted to be independent financially. Even though I can't be independent physically, I felt that in one part of my life I could be independent.

Another thing about working is, it keeps me so busy I don't have time to feel sorry for myself. I don't have aches or pains. I don't have time for them.

To move ahead with our lives and dreams, we have to accept the cards we've been handed. What did accepting your condition do for you?

You gain a feeling that you have surmounted or gone beyond it. At first you go through the usual stages—grief, anger, denial—then you finally reach acceptance. You realize that, "Hey, this is what I have to deal with" and you do it. You can't just keep being angry. People have said, "You always have a smile on your face, you are always cheerful and you don't complain." That is the way I have tried to be, although I do have my bad days like everyone else.

It seems that our dreams are never completely our own. We must always have help in attaining them. In your quest, you've found you must depend on others and you've come to accept that.

When I broke my hip in 1991, I had to rely on nurse's aides for help getting up and getting into bed. At first I resented them for being there, but I knew that in order to get out and go to work, I needed their help. So yes, here I was, even more dependent—but with their help I could get up, get dressed and go out to work, church and dinner. So, yes, I can be independent and still rely on others.

Relying on them and being dependent on them gives me the opportunity to be independent in other parts of my life. And no, none of us can be completely independent—unless we live alone on an island, I guess. In today's world, we all depend on one another. We can be independent as far as taking care of ourselves by having our own job and own home, but we also need people—our family and our friends—to lean on for support, for companionship.

You'll achieve another dream shortly when you finish your college degree in adult education. We know that you don't plan to teach, so what does earning this degree mean to you?

It is a piece of paper I've wanted since I was 18. It represents the fact that I was determined to get it.

What will you do to celebrate?

Have a big party! I'm inviting everyone I know and if they can come, fine. If they can't come, fine. It is a good excuse to get together—like Christmas or Thanksgiving.

What does success mean to you, and how have your views of success and its meaning changed over the years?

Success at first was more monetary. It meant making a lot of money. But now it isn't. Now, it is having the money to be independent. Success, to me, is to be independent. And while, as I said, I can't be independent physically, I can be independent financially, and that gives me a great deal of satisfaction. For right now, my kids or nobody else has to help me. I've got some savings, and I'll have my retirement—so hopefully I'll be able to manage. I'll find a way.

Jack Canfield, co-author of the best-selling *Chicken Soup for the Soul* series of books that have helped activate the dreams of millions.

14

JACK CANFIELD
AUTHOR, TEACHER,
CHICKEN SOUP CONNOISSEUR

"We only grow from the truth."

What do you think of when you hear the words "chicken soup"?

A dozen years ago, chances are you would have visualized a certain red and white can. But since that time, another cultural icon has gained a foothold in our consciousness—the *Chicken Soup for the Soul®* series of books and products. The first book has sold more than seven million copies in 20 languages, the books in the series have sold more than 28 million copies and at one point in 1998, five of the top 10 slots on the national paperback bestseller list were occupied by *Chicken Soup* titles. There's no slowing down, either. Plans call for at least 30 more titles in the series over the next few years, aimed at every kind of soul one can imagine.

Making those plans are the series co-authors, Mark Victor Hansen and Jack Canfield, who met each other at a holistic health conference in the mid-1980s. Both before and since that meeting, they have dedicated their lives to enhancing the personal and professional development of people all over the world. Through such ventures as Self-Esteem Seminars, The Canfield Group and The Foundation for Self-Esteem, Jack Canfield has been recognized as one of the world's foremost authorities on self-esteem and peak performance training.

Like most overnight successes, however, there's nothing overnight about it. Many are familiar with the story of the first *Chicken Soup* book—how the authors persevered through 33 rejections before Health Communications, Inc., decided to take a chance and publish it, in the hopes of selling maybe 20,000 copies. The unprecedented success since then is a tribute not only to tenacity, but to positive visualization.

"When we were trying to sell that book," says Canfield, "we cut out a copy of the *New York Times* bestseller list, whited out the current 'number one' title and pasted our book title in its place."

Jack Canfield has been helping people see bright futures for a long time. His career as a motivator began in tough territory—as a history teacher in an inner-city high school in Chicago.

"I realized that I was more interested in why kids weren't learning than in teaching history," he said in a 1999 *Writer's Digest* article. Soon thereafter, he hooked up with W. Clement Stone, founder of *Success* magazine. What Jack learned from Stone launched him on his new mission of training teachers, helping both them and their students reach higher levels of achievement through personal responsibility and service.

Jack has been a university teacher, a trainer and a successful psychotherapist. He and his colleagues have trained and consulted for companies such as GE, NCR, Scott Paper, Clairol, Johnson & Johnson . . . and even Campbell Soup. As a highly sought-after speaker, Jack is known for his powerful, dynamic and entertaining style, automatically engaging his audiences and, more often than not, transforming them.

His quest is a spiritual one, a mission to discover and share the capabilities of our higher selves, to uncover the spiritual dimension of our daily lives and bring that energy into our work, our families, our relationships—and, yes, our dreams.

Successful pursuit of vision is a big part of that mission, whether for an individual or an organization. Often, in a corporate setting, Jack brings his insight and positive outlook to bear on a specific company's strengths and weaknesses, facilitating discovery and resolution of issues that may be hampering production or stymieing creativity.

Among the many exercises Canfield has employed is an "act as if" cocktail party. As he puts it, "You train people how to treat you by how you treat yourself." In this exercise, if you could be in any position in your organization, you act as if you're already that person. What Canfield has observed in people time and again is changing postures, more assertive voices, more eye contact and a general air of self-confidence. People's images of themselves actually change with just a little imagination. "You become who you act as if you are," he says.

Similarly, if we act as if we're going after a dream, that may well be the first step in getting there.

Jack has learned a lot from the teachings of Moshe Feldenkrais, whose ideas on body awareness and movement can help a person align himself with his unconscious—with his dreams and visions. With organizational vision, the body's counterpart might involve everything from the physical plant to the supply chain flow chart. "Body," after all, is the root of "corporation."

Through such techniques, Jack helps people and companies get at the roots of themselves, the truth of their enterprises and lives. One of his favorite slogans, plastered on office walls at *Chicken Soup* headquarters in Santa Barbara, California, is "Tell the truth faster." In other words, when we are behaving in a fully integrated way, the truth of who we are becomes immediately apparent, sparking positive and productive action.

Some of us might be afraid to uncover such power. But telling our truth faster can allow us to realize our dreams faster too. And if articulation is the first step toward realization, well, our souls might be fed like never before.

A CONVERSATION WITH JACK CANFIELD . . .

One of the chief elements in your live presentations is the development of a clear and detailed vision. Is that something that people often don't do thoroughly enough?

I take people through the 10 steps to success, and the most important exercises have to do with developing clear vision, how to get to what your vision is and turn it into specific objectives and goals. Most people don't do that properly.

People don't get specific enough. They may say, "My goal is to have a house on the ocean." Well, how much of a house? By when? On what ocean? You may want to reduce turnover, raise reading scores or increase sales. Well, by what date do you want to double your sales?

Through this process, people make their goals smaller and put them farther out in time. As soon as you commit to a specific time and place, it brings up fears, considerations, and roadblocks. You don't want to sacrifice your family life, for example, or you don't want to ask for money.

Most people will not commit to something if they don't see how they can do it. Our unconscious mind is the problem solver, but it doesn't go to work until you commit to a specific goal. Let's say you want to make $100,000. You might initially say you couldn't do it. But as soon as you commit to a goal, as if it's already achieved, that activates the subconscious mind to come up with a solution.

For instance, while in the shower you might think of putting together a book of other people's writing. Now, I couldn't possibly write 101 stories eight times a year. But as soon as you commit to the goal, and visualize it twice a day in alpha brain wave state, you're programming that part of the brain called the reticular activating system, and it frees up creativity. You're not thinking of your right foot, but as soon as I say it you feel it. Most of the time, you're filtering out the majority of everything available to your consciousness. But if you set that goal, the filter opens up.

People like Bill Gates and Michael Dell see things differently than everyone else does. And once you see how to do it, you can't *not* see how to do it. You get there, and your self-image shifts. Most people stay stuck in the same level and lifestyle their whole lives. But others find this sense of belief and make things possible.

What is the role of imagination in the workplace?

I see two functions of the imagination. First, we think in sounds and pictures, which correspond to words and imagination. And we think with our feelings. I talk about directive and receptive imagery. The directive is the goal setting part. The receptive imagery is about finding answers. Let's say we're stuck and can't figure out the answer to a question. You close your eyes, go inside and find an image to help solve it.

Many years ago, a question in a workshop I was taking was, "What's the next step in your personal growth?" I immediately saw a bulldozer and a field of aspens. Then those things were on my desk, pushing off papers. I realized that I wasn't spending enough time with people and I needed less time with paper shuffling.

You can program images into the unconscious which affect your willpower. Whatever image you're holding in your head is what your body will create. If you only want to make $36,000 a year, that's what you will create. I learned it from Moshe Feldenkrais, an Israeli who is a ground breaker in the arena of working with the body. He was a judo expert who almost became paralyzed and worked his way back to championship level. He understood how to use the mind to relax the body, to create an image for the body to move into.

You are a pioneer in the area of self-esteem. How are self-esteem and the concept of emotional intelligence related?

Certain people have highly developed empathy skills. If other people start to tear up, swallow, fold their arms . . . they pick up on those signals. Naturally empathic people become teachers, therapists, that kind of work. Some people are not empathic. I used to get shocked at how insensitive a guy I worked with was. He wouldn't even notice it.

There are two elements—sensing other people's emotions, and understanding them. Then knowing and understanding your own feelings. I've been in therapy for 20 years. I'm constantly learning how to better deal with my own emotions. Yesterday, for instance, I was complaining about my partner. But it was not my partner who was frustrating me, it was my own expectations. As I looked deeper, I saw that it would have been easy to make him look wrong and then get people to agree with me, but the better idea is to confront my partner. I'd have to stand up to him—and I was never able to stand up to my dad.

Emotional intelligence would give you a place where you can withdraw, and you can see what's going on. I have to stand up and say I don't want to do that, and risk people not liking me.

I have a friend named Norman Howell, who owns a company with about 40 employees. They go to EST training and they take my self-esteem training. They devise a personal stretch goal every month and receive a five percent bonus for every stretch they complete. Sometimes they put themselves at risk—everything from sleeping outside with the homeless to singing a song in front of a group, giving $100 to charity and justifying it to the group, or painting a Habitat for Humanity house.

One thing they do is to spend a day together in isolation. No journal writing, no TV or movies, nothing. It's a very confrontational atmosphere. People can get bored, antsy and irritated, but they finally get calmed down. You realize there's nowhere to go. These people are clear about their feelings. They're open with their clients, and you can't con them. They're articulate and self-assertive.

You may not be able to pull that off with a huge company. But that kind of commitment pays off for Norman. He probably "hundred percents" himself every year.

How can leaders, who often lead best by intuition, learn to trust the intuition of their employees?

Actually, I don't know a lot of people who have been successful at doing that. It seems like visionary leaders tend to surround themselves with detail people. Visionaries don't need visionaries around them. Mark Victor Hansen is a visionary who's like a 10, and I'm more like a five. You can't have an organization full of visionaries.

Your method and your message rely on the extraordinary power of story, on the literal "word of mouth." Other than in forums like your books, where are people finding the opportunities to tell these stories? Have you encountered specific organizations where that "telling" is paramount?

There's not a lot of that. There are two kinds of stories: daily stories and metastories. For instance, early in his life George Washington attacked a group and accidentally killed an ambassador. If his metastory was, "I'm a loser and I don't do anything right," his place in history would be different than if he said, "I want to make a difference in the world." If a person is an alcoholic, they can define themselves that way or they can decide that their metastory is "I was born to have a higher purpose."

People's daily stories are justifications of their larger metastories. Blamers and complainers blame and complain. Motivators and inspirers tell stories like that. My colleague Martin Rutte has created Chicken Soup at Work groups. The concept is the cheapest form of internal consulting you can get: Buy everyone a *Chicken Soup for the Soul at Work* book, come to work the next day, and instead of talking about sports, we talk about what story we read that affected us the most, and what we could do to bring the quality of that story into our work experience. They're doing this at Southwest Airlines, PG&E, and some other Fortune 100 companies. Martin got people talking about these stories. And very powerful things begin to happen.

Any good CEO is a good motivator, and good CEOs tell stories. They tell about what's possible, like a good coach—

"Back in 1962, we were down by 32 points and we came back to win." All good leaders are good storytellers.

One story that refuses to go away is the state of our nation's children. After all the school violence over the past several years, some people are in a state of near panic about the psychological health and self-esteem of young people. What has been your experience of America's youth, and how have you addressed self-esteem concerns in light of this disturbing course of events?

To me it's been totally avoidable. I was on a panel recently, and I said that I knew what to do—we had gangs back in Chicago who wanted to go to war.

We have alienated kids who feel unconnected to anybody, whether it's family, other kids or people at school. What solves that is inclusion. The basic building block of self-esteem education, holistic education, character building or violence prevention is getting kids to talk to each other about things that matter. You start by breaking them into pairs: talk about making friends, what they do when they're lonely, their biggest fears, their dreams, how they get along with their families. They can switch roles.

There are kids who don't get attention for even two minutes all day in school. They never participate. So you break them into groups of six, and they can only talk while they're holding a baseball, talking about things that are emotionally significant in their lives. That way, they get experience at dealing with this kind of thing.

Harry Stack Sullivan said kids suffer from the "delusion of uniqueness." They think they're the only one with zits. If you could just have a program every day for a half-hour called Self Science 101—"How do I study me, how do I learn to express my feelings, express my sadness?" Kids are not learning the basic social, psychological tools they need to negotiate their emotions.

To me it's simple. In grad school in 1968 we were teaching this stuff to teachers. People resisted because it's uncomfortable. They don't want their private lives in public. So you get all this pressure based on fear. People pull away and you get fear.

There's one exercise called "Secrets," where for two hours we share our secrets. By the end of two hours people realize, "Hey, we all have done this stuff. I don't need to beat myself up. We all feel alienated, afraid of rejection. I'm not alone. I can learn, and move on."

What was the catalyst for your dream to spread your stories through the *Chicken Soup* series? Was it allowing spiritual and emotional energies to enter into your professional, working life?

I may appear in public with my Mont Blanc pen and Armani suit, but when I tell my truth—when I share that my oldest son is in a rehab center, and my mother had a heart attack, when my wife and I are having challenging times, or I talk about my fear of aging and how my knees hurt when I run—people feel closer to me and give me more leverage to have an impact in their lives.

So I have a phrase: "Tell the truth faster." We only grow from the truth. We don't want to admit that we screwed up. We're afraid to share because we're afraid people will judge us. But self-disclosure, vulnerability and honesty are crucial. I was scared to do it, but I survived it and now there's very little I wouldn't tell anyone on the planet.

A defining moment for me was understanding that I couldn't separate my spiritual life from my professional life. I didn't want to be seen as "California"—flaky, New Age—but as a solid business person so people would respect me. But the more I discovered, the more I saw that the things that were good management were things taught in the Bible, in Taoism, in Buddhism and other traditions. I began to share readings from different spiritual books. People *want* to talk about spiritual values. They don't want their work to be devoid of caring, love and compassion.

That happened about 13 years ago. Dealing with your highest self is dealing with your own soul. That's what led to the *Chicken Soup for the Soul* books. They evoke an inner commitment in people to want to have those kinds of experiences in their own lives. The stories gave them permission to open up in the face of obstacles, to go after their own goals.